THE WOOD LIFE

THE WOOD LIFE

By MARK WOOD

with Vithushan Ehantharajah

ALLEN&UNWIN

First published in hardback in Great Britain in 2022 by Allen & Unwin,
an imprint of Atlantic Books Ltd.

This paperback edition published in 2023 by Allen & Unwin,
an imprint of Atlantic Books.

Plate section photography credits: Page 2 – middle photograph by
Justin Tallis/Getty Images, bottom photograph by Gareth Copley/Getty
Images; Page 3 – top and middle photographs by Randy Brooks/Getty
Images; Page 4 – bottom photograph by Gareth Copley-ICC/Getty
Images; Page 5 – top photograph by Clive Mason/Getty Images;
all other featured images courtesy of the author.

Every efforthasbeenmadetotraceorcontactallcopyrightholders.
The publishers will be pleased to make good any omissions or rectify
any mistakes brought to their attention at the earliest opportunity.

10 9 8 7 6 5 4 3 2

A CIP catalogue record for this book is available from the British Library.

Paperback ISBN: 978 1 83895 582 3
E-book ISBN: 978 1 83895 581 6

Printed in Great Britain by CPI Group (UK) Ltd, Croydon CR0 4YY

Allen & Unwin
An imprint of Atlantic Books Ltd
Ormond House
26–27 Boswell Street
London
WC1N 3JZ

www.atlantic-books.co.uk

To Mam, Dad, Sarah, Harry and
Ashington Cricket Club

CONTENTS

Foreword by Ben Stokes   ix

Introduction   1

1   How to Celebrate   7

2   How to Kill Time   37

3   How to Be Fast   73

4   How to Love   111

5   How to Travel   143

6   How to Stay Healthy   179

7   How to Keep Level   209

8   How to Be True to Yourself   245

9   Q & A   269

Epilogue: Mark Wood, A Second Opinion
    by Miles Jupp   283

Foreword

by Ben Stokes

People always ask me what Mark Wood is like. Not so much the player, because you can tell what fast bowlers are like pretty easily. They're not the most sophisticated. But people are always fascinated by Mark Wood, the person. I'm probably quite well placed to give them an answer because of how long we have known each other.

The first time I remember us coming across each other was when he was playing for Northumberland and I was playing for Cumbria. Apparently, we also played club cricket against each other at a competition in York, him and his Ashington boys against my side, Cockermouth. We won, of course. The first time we spent time together properly, though, was in the Durham Academy. Woody was the year above me, so he was sixteen and I was a year younger. Then, fifteen years later, we've played together for Durham first team, and are teammates with

England in all three formats. All while becoming best mates.

When I think about all that time we've spent together, my answer about what Woody is like is simple: he's been the same throughout. What you see as a thirty-two-year-old is what he was like as a sixteen-year-old. Though I'm not sure which way around is worse – the fact he was the same at sixteen as he is at thirty-two or the same at thirty-two as he was at sixteen? Either way, it's why we get on.

What you see is what you get with Woody. He was always the joker of the class. The clown who was always making people laugh and not taking things outside of cricket too seriously. But when it came to cricket, he turned it on but still always had the enjoyment, trying to make it fun for himself and everyone around him.

The first time I played Minor Counties cricket against him, he was a middle-order batter and bowled little mediums, which shows how times have changed. Because he's definitely not a middle-order batter now. To be fair, he's not a medium pacer either. I think there was a stage at the academy when I might have bowled a bit quicker than him. Then he started bowling rockets and didn't look back.

When you progress through the ranks and end up with the greatest honour, that is to represent your country, you're going to play with a lot of people because the nature of that level is that people for any number of reasons come in and out of the team. So it's always special that me and

Woody have been able to do it at the highest level with people that we grew up playing with – both each other and from an age-group point of view as well.

I remember when I gave Woody his fiftieth ODI cap, which was the semi-final of the 2019 World Cup against Australia. For milestones like that, very often an ex-player hands over the cap. But as someone who has been close to Woody for so long, when Eoin Morgan asked me to do the honours, I said absolutely.

Not too many people would know the ins and outs of Woody's career when it came to the challenges he has overcome. I probably know more than most about how the injury side has affected him. Two years before the World Cup there was a time when – he won't mind me saying – he was at a real low point. It's not as simple as 'Oh, he's injured again.' There are a lot of deeper things like that with what Woody went through: it's your confidence in your body, it's the afterthought of 'How many games can I put together?' Or, 'If I have one more injury, is that going to be it?' It's not as simple as an 'injury', if that makes sense. There's so much more to it. Knowing how that affected him, and then to see him where he was when I was giving him his fiftieth cap, was something I had to mention because it was more than playing fifty games for England, it's everything else he had been through on the ride to get here.

When you've been on the journey Woody and I had to get here for England, you can't not think about all the other things we've been through on the way. Because it's not normal, is it? Or rather, it's not given. From being fifteen and playing together to being in our thirties representing England in a World Cup, there's so much that goes on between us.

I want to say I knew to say all that off the top of my head when I gave him the cap, but I actually had notes written down on the palm of my hand so I didn't forget anything. I had little bullet points in ballpoint pen written down.

MARK WOOD: *Sorry to interrupt, Stokesy, especially where you're being so nice about us. But did you have to write them at a funny angle because of your broken fingers?*

Aye, I did. But that's the thing, I had to make sure I got it right, said everything I needed to say. It meant a lot to you, and it also meant a lot to me. It was great I could be a part of that special moment. I've been part of other moments with Woody as well for England.

You know when they say you're a product of your environment and how you've been raised? Well, Woody is the epitome of that.

Whenever Woody and I were travelling, Woody's mam would always buy Percy Pigs because she knows I like Percy Pigs. Woody does that for other people – he's always looking out for other people. He'll always know if someone is ill and his first reaction is 'Ah, right, I'll go to the shop and get them this.'

He's a very generous person, very thoughtful and one of the guys who will always look after his peers. Which in a way is weird because he is one of the tightest people with money I've ever met. For example, whenever we'd do something together, like going for a bit of an adventure, a walk or something social when we're on tour, he'd come out and you could tell he was just in sponsor's gear, head to toe in New Balance or England kit. I'd have to ask: 'Woody, is anything you're wearing paid for?' And the answer was always 'Nah.'

As for a self-help book, I was a bit surprised when Woody told us that he was doing one. But, thinking about it, I don't know that there's a better cricketer to write one than Woody.

There are always those people you've got to feel comfortable going to for advice, especially when it's serious. For Woody, as someone I spend so much time with, it's natural. One thing he's always been very good at, especially when I've grown as a more senior player, is reassuring me. Whenever I speak, and it's not something I do particularly often, he'll always come over and say, 'Ah, mate, that was mint.' I would say he gives everybody that kind of reassurance.

Come to think of it, the best bit of advice I've ever been given was from Woody.

One night I fell asleep with chewing gum in my mouth and woke up with the chewing gum stuck in my hair.

He was the first person I had to get to: 'Woody, I've got chewing gum in my hair!' I was thinking, 'Oh no, I'm going to have to freeze it, I'm going to need to do all sorts.' Then Woody rang Sarah and she calmly said, 'Oh aye, just put conditioner in it and it will just fall out.' I was like, 'Give over, that is not going to work. No chance. Absolute rubbish.' And it worked! Chewing gum out of the hair. Amazing. To this day, I think that's still the best piece of advice I've been given.

MARK WOOD: *I mean, technically that didn't come from me, so I don't know if I can claim credit for that. But I'll take it. More nuggets this way...*

INTRODUCTION

Self-help books have always fascinated us. I mean, it's kind of weird as a concept, right? 'Here's what you need to do to be a better person.' It's quite a big claim to say you've got all the answers to life's questions. Everyone's different, everyone has their own lives and what they want to achieve from them. Not everyone likes the same old thing. We're all unique, and all have different tastes. It's like what they say about Bovril or Marmite – you either like it or you're wrong.

Hallo – I'm Mark Wood, by the way. Probably should have started with that. There's your first lesson: always introduce yourself first.

As an England and Durham cricketer who was born, raised and refined in Ashington, Northumberland, my life has been quite unique. Over the course of my career so far, I've won an Ashes and a World Cup in an international career that at the time of writing is going on seven years and counting.

Being a fast bowler like myself is up there with the toughest of all sporting pursuits, like being Tyson Fury's punchbag or working behind the bar during the darts at Ally Pally.

Being a cricketer? There's nothing like it. And doing it for England? Well, I'm lucky to call it a profession. There's been a lot of hard work along the way. Plenty of sacrifices and pain to accompany the good times that make them all worthwhile.

I've been everywhere, from Barbados to Brisbane, Chester-le-Street to Chennai, waiting rooms to operating tables. I've played in some of the most exotic locations in the world and eaten margherita pizzas in every single one of them. To be honest, it's amazing I've waited this long to bring out my own self-help book.

I don't claim to have all the answers. I'm still trying to work some of them out myself, to be honest. And writing this book has definitely got me closer to a few of them.

The answers I do have are probably to questions you never really thought of asking. What does it feel like to bowl over 90 miles an hour? How do you have a great time without alcohol? How do you overcome nerves to give some of the best wedding speeches ever heard in the north-east of England? Why does Joe Root need so many bats? And how do you successfully raise, flog (and later put down) an imaginary horse? Well, you've picked up the right book.

Cards on the table, you are likely to get to the end of this book and not learn much useful at all. Certainly not much you'll be able to put into practice. There's only so much I'm going to be able to teach you. Some of it you'll already know, like how Ferrero Rochers are mankind's greatest achievement and that you should never sit next to Ben Stokes on a bumpy flight. At the very least you might get a few laughs at my expense.

Perhaps this is more of a 'not-so-helpful self-help book'. There really should be more of those. 'Here's how I cocked up.' I'd read that all day. Because we make mistakes all the time, don't we? Mistakes are what make us human. Hopefully this book isn't one of them, mind.

Throughout these pages, important people from my life will drop in to tell you their side of my story. The reason I am in the position I'm in is down to many who have helped me over the years and those who supported and believed in my ability and in me as a person, throughout. I'll be honest with you, though: take what some of them say with a pinch of salt. Especially my lifelong mates Jonny Storey, Scott Dunn, Glen Taylor and Daniel Grant, my England colleagues Jos Buttler and Chris Woakes. Oh, and my parents, Derek and Angela Wood. Apart from when they say nice stuff about us. In fact, all the nice stuff is true. Hope that helps.

I should also say, in lieu of a glossary, there will be some moments that might jar if you're not from these parts. At times I'll use 'us' instead of 'me'. 'Gan' means 'go', 'mint' can mean either 'good' or 'great'. The word 'canny' is just as versatile – 'good', 'lovely' and even chucked in front of the word 'mint' to say something's really good. And, of course, 'ha-way' or 'h'way', which can mean 'come on' in a positive way – 'ha-way the lads' – or negatively, like 'ha-way man, what are you playing at?!'

Anything I've missed should be self-explanatory. By the end of this book, you should learn a bit more about me, pick up a few life lessons and feel comfortable walking into Toon (town) and ordering a ham and pease pudding sandwich with a pint of Newcy Brown (or lemonade).

With that, enjoy, and welcome to *The Wood Life*.

1

HOW TO CELEBRATE

Contrary to popular belief, you don't need alcohol to celebrate. I would know. I don't touch the stuff.

No one seems to believe me. Maybe it's because of how I am naturally, people just assume I'm always high on something. But I've never needed or wanted it.

Not everyone knows what to do with that information. Whenever I'm in a bar, folk will come up being nice and ask to get me something. 'What are you drinking?' Water, please. 'Woody's so funny! What is he like?!' No, seriously, I'm drinking water. 'Ha, what a lad. What is it?' Seriously, just water's fine. 'Ah, he's on the vodka, isn't he?'

When I was playing club cricket in Australia, I went into this pub that was serving all your Aussie staples: Queensland's XXXX, Victoria Bitter – all the beers you see on playing shirts. Then I saw a woman at the bar nursing this red drink. I asked her what it was: raspberry lemonade, which sounded quite nice.

'Barman, can I get one of these raspberry lemonades?' He stopped dead and looked me up and down: 'You OK, mate?' 'Ermmm, yeah, fine pal. I just want a raspberry lemonade.'

It's not a religious thing either. I just can't stand the stuff.

It all started as a fourteen-year-old at a house party in Ashington with my mates and this lass who I quite fancied. It was my first proper house party as well, so I'm trying to act cool – like I do this all the time.

Anyway, this lass, I don't know if she fancied me, but she was like, 'If you neck this beer, I'll take my top off.' Obviously, I go to neck it – my first ever beer. Obviously, I don't neck it. Obviously, I'm then sick everywhere and have to leave out of embarrassment.

Ever since, I've hated the taste. Honestly, hate it. I don't think there's anything that tastes worse on the planet. I suppose though the hate goes a bit deeper than the taste with it having those bad memories for me as a kid.

My next and definitely final beer came when we won the 2019 World Cup. Not by choice, mind. For the whole build-up to the final, Stokesy was on at me. Even on the morning of the game, he wouldn't let it go.

'If we win, you have to have a beer!' I kept telling him 'ner, man', but he wouldn't listen. He's not an easy man to say no to and this was not something I was going to budge on, so we went around and around. In the end, I was sick of him going on about it, so I agreed.

Didn't let me forget, did he? That Sunday night, we're all in the changing room and Stokesy collars me, hands me a beer and says, 'Right – see that off.' I start getting flashbacks. Even the smell. God – how can you? Any of you? It's vile. But given we wouldn't be there celebrating a historic win without him, I suppose I can do this for him.

I nursed it for three hours, so it was basically 30 degrees when I eventually finished it. Proud – and a bit sick – I went over to Stokesy and said, 'There you go,' handing him the empty bottle. Of course, he had no clue what I was on about – he was a few sheets to the wind at this point. Understandably so.

BEN STOKES: *Right, I've got to jump in here because that's not exactly how I put it. I said if we win this World Cup, I want to share a beer with you. I didn't force it down you!*

MARK WOOD: *Aye, that's fair.*

STOKES: *But it was surreal anyway, because I had Woody drinking a beer at the World Cup final, and then Woody's mother was nursing my daughter, Livy, who was only four or five at the time. She was feeding her Powerade. The kids were just running wild and I walked in and see Woody's mam dripping blue Powerade into Livy's mouth because she wanted a drink. I just remember thinking, 'This is mint!'*

WOOD: *Good old Angela. Always good with the kids.*

I had to wash the taste out with something. Luckily, we had this fridge full of still and sparking water. I cracked through those and, when that was done, had a couple of Powerades. I know, I know, mixing my drinks until 3 a.m. What an animal!

The next day there was a function at The Oval to meet the fans. Stokesy hadn't slept by the time we set off for the event. There's a great picture of all the lads with their tired eyes and shades while me, Adil Rashid and Moeen Ali were fresh as daisies while thousands of kids were running around screaming.

The great thing about celebrating wins in cricket is that it doesn't change the further up you go. Even after an incredible win like that, the changing room is always the place to be.

After beating New Zealand in that nail-biter, we all celebrated in the pavilion with friends and family. We then made our way back up to the changing room, where Jos Buttler had written the lyrics to the victory song he and I had come up with on his match bat.

It's the Liverpool 'Allez' song. Our version goes like this:

We've conquered all the world
We're never gonna stop
From Lord's down to Sydney
We've won the bloomin' lot
Our heartbeat is Mark Saxby
Our captain is Morgan
Taking the cap forward
As the World Champions
Allez allez allez!

Mark Saxby is the team's support coach. His official title is 'team masseur' but he does every little job. He goes out of his way to do all the little things, whether that's filling water bottles or tidying up – things we should do ourselves, really. He keeps morale up and keeps people grounded. He's funny, genuine and very trusted – there's nothing he doesn't know about us. It's a bit like a hairdresser: you get chatting idly while getting a rub-down and before you know it you've unloaded everything about your life onto him, and feel better for it. He really is our heartbeat.

We must have sung that song a hundred times. We sang another one about Jos as well, to the tune of 'Feeling Hot Hot Hot':

Jose, Jose...
Jose, Jose...
Jossy But-But-ler!

Not quite as lyrically challenging, but fun to sing all the same. There's a Stokesy chant as well, to the tune of 'Three Lions'. I came up with it, but I can't print it. Maybe in my next book, when we're all old, fat and retired. We'll see.

Cricket's one of those sports where there are a lot of opportunities to celebrate. In football or rugby, you score a goal or a try and go big. In cricket, you've got wickets, fifties, hundreds, catches and run-outs – plenty of moments when you can go big. Lots of bowlers have pre-planned celebrations to wickets, like Sheldon Cottrell's salute, Shahid Afridi's Starman pose or Hasan Ali's punch the ground and explode up, but I've never thought about having a pre-planned one. I'm not the type. More often than not I'm just thrilled I've managed to take a wicket and so I run around screaming like a loony. For a while Joe Root and I did this American Football-style jump into each other whenever one of us did something in an ODI. I think we did it first off-the-cuff in a football warm-up and thought, right, that's cool, let's do that again when one of us does something good on the pitch. But we've not done it recently because I think we both forgot.

★

One of the greatest things about cricket culture is it doesn't change, whether you're in a club third XI or playing for England. Provided you're around the teammates you grafted with – in victory and defeat – the vibes and traditions remain the same. One of those traditions that carries on all the way to the top is the fines meeting.

To those of you who play the game, this will require no further explanation. To those who don't, it's essentially a score-settling exercise. Over the course of a season or series, the team keeps notes of anyone who's stepped out of line. At the end, you all get together and hand out 'fines'. The punishments are passed down by the designated 'fines masters'. All teams have them, and grassing on your team-mates is encouraged. And for better or worse in my case, the fines are usually alcohol-based.

Back home at Ashington, when I played for Ashington Cricket Club in the Northumberland and Tyneside League, this ceremony was known as the Kangaroo Court. There were two categories in particular you wanted to avoid: the 'Bobby Boot' and 'Bobby Box' award. Look away from the next paragraph if you have a weak stomach.

So, this is named after this club legend, Bob the Dog – Paul 'Bob' Rutherford. He is the slowest slow-left arm bowler anybody would ever face. He also doesn't shower properly, wears the same clothes every day of his life. Great character but a total mess when it comes to hygiene. Anyway, as you may have guessed, the worst punishment handed down there is having to drink out of Bobby's shoe or box. Thankfully, for England you just have to neck what's in your hand.

You can be fined for just about anything. The more ridiculous the reason, the better.

I used to get fined for being the richest man in Ashington. For being best friends with my uncle Neil because I used to follow him around like a shadow. For being half as good as Toby Roland-Jones. For being half as good as Jofra Archer. For being half as good as Olly Stone. Basically, every time a new fast bowler comes on the scene, I get fined.

The fines are just as daft at international level and sometimes we meet up with the other side to do our meetings together, which is a brilliant way to mend relationships after a hard-fought scrap. This was the case after the South Africa tour in 2020, with the designated fines masters Jos Buttler and Rassie van der Dussen.

Rassie gave the first one to Stokesy because he had been sledging him all tour, but had been getting it slightly wrong each time. So Rassie got some payback: 'I'd like to give this first one to Ben. He's called me a German all series even though my family is Dutch!' Yes, that's right, Stoksey thought someone with the last name 'van der Dussen' was German not Dutch.

The support staff are fair game, too. Our batting coaches Jacques Kallis and Graham Thorpe were both fined for being Advanced Hair Studio's number-one clients. They had to do a 'rug-off', which was basically a 'boat race': who could neck their drink quickest. Thorpey's pretty good but Kallis's hands, head, shoulders, neck and pecs are just bigger and he almost swallowed the bottle whole to win impressively.

Now, I know what you're thinking: 'Woody, you don't drink!' But that doesn't mean I'm safe. Far from it. The number of times I've had to knock back a concoction of sports drink, Coke, Red Bull and, often, deodorant. I just close me eyes and hoy it down me throat!

If you're like me and this doesn't sound like the thing for

you, I've got some tips to help you get by and navigate the peer pressure.

Over the years I've managed to create my own role in fines meetings. At Durham, I created the role of 'pourer' where I'd make sure everyone's drinks are topped up.

Every now and again I might say something to the fines master like, 'Oh, this guy did this during the season.' I'm like the hand of the king in *Game of Thrones*: I'm manipulative, sly and conniving. Basically, grassing on everybody. Remember, this isn't *The Sopranos*, so ratting on your teammates is fair game. I also used it as an opportunity to get things off my chest that I'd been carrying all season.

One year, Gareth Harte, a batter at Durham, had been winding us up constantly, particularly about my shoes. This one occasion he took the laces out, thinking he was clever. The kind of nonsense that you grow out of at school but still carries on in sporting dressing rooms. Sick of him, I decided to put some 'foreign' liquid in the spray-on sun cream. I told my teammate Graham Clark about it and we kept it quiet right the way through the summer, trying to keep a straight face as he layered up to cope with the harsh sunshine of the north-east of England.

It wasn't until the fines meeting at the end of that season that I told him what I'd done. Luckily, he just embraced it. I'm not sure if he would have done had I told him at any other time. He's a great lad – a South African too, and luckily South Africans always make sure they're sorted before anyone else, so no one was in any danger of borrowing my awful concoction. I wasn't proud of it, so it was great to get it out in the open and off my chest.

You get to the point of no return with this kind of do. It's not too different when you're on a night out and people start going over the edge from fun-drunk tipsy to being annoying and bothering you. It's probably like what I am to them when I'm sober. I reckon I am one of the best drunk actors in the world: the number of times I've managed to act like I'm losing my bearings or slur my speech to avoid a round of shots and what-not are too many to count. I should win Oscars for it. But when it gets to that where it's too much to handle, that's when I make my excuses and leave. Say farewell to a couple of people but not too many and slink out. The Irish Goodbye – or The Woody Goodbye, as it should now be known.

★

Thankfully, the changing room isn't all lads and mickey-taking. Just as important as celebrating the wins is letting them sink in. The changing room is a private place that has an array of emotions over the course of a game, whether a five-day Test or the few hours of a Twenty20. It can be both angry and quiet after defeat, and loud and contemplative in victory. It's a place where you can also feel at ease, and often the more subdued moments are the ones that stick with you.

After that series win in South Africa, we got the ex-players to come in to celebrate with us, which included the guys from talkSPORT who were covering it on radio. I've known Stephen Harmison for years: he was a great help to me when I was coming through at Durham, and always supportive of me. He was always giving me praise in the media as well, which helps any player.

I took nine wickets in the final Test at Johannesburg, which helped us take the series 3–1: five in the first innings, then four in the second to get us over the line. It was pretty satisfying all round, especially getting van der Dussen caught at cover for 98. We set a short-ball field around the wicket. I bowled a couple of bouncers and figured I'd press the gamble button and pitch one up. I was thinking more he'd nick it than pan it straight to Stuart Broad. But that was particularly pleasing because he was getting under our skin a bit at the time. Just loads of sledging when we were batting. Constantly going on and on. It's probably why he made a good fines master.

At the end of the game, Harmy was the first to give me a big hug and tell me it was what I deserved. Darren Gough came up to me and said, 'Well done, I'm really proud of you.' I was over the moon. He was someone whose action I tried to copy in the back garden more than anyone. I couldn't believe he'd said that to me. I really loved that. Just having them all there, it was awesome.

St Lucia in 2019, though, was something special: I cried

my eyes out when the Test was over. It's the only time I've been emotional over cricket, really.

It was here I took my first five-wicket haul. The Barmy Army were all there, singing about me. I'd taken the last wicket of the West Indies' first innings and had all kinds of emotion going through me as I walked off, holding the ball up to salute the crowds. Broady actually got the ball for us after I had bowled Shannon Gabriel. I was getting hugs from everyone and, as we walked off, Broady put his arm around my shoulder and handed it to me. He knew it was something I should keep hold of. He would know, given he's taken nineteen of them. I kissed the ball and then held it straight up in the air and waved it around.

When I got into the dressing room, everyone was clapping as I came in. I hugged the physio and I remember feeling overwhelmed with relief, due to the fact that I'd finally taken a five-wicket haul in a Test, having shown all this potential but never being able to quite live up to it due to my body breaking down time and again. I was welling up and was struggling to hold it together. Then Jimmy saw me and went, 'Ah, come on, mate,' and hugged me and I let it all out.

I'd like to say most of the winning is celebrated gracefully. But there are times when you've beaten a rival and want to rub it in. And that's OK in my book.

Before the 2015 Ashes there was this video doing the rounds of Shane Watson and Steve Smith speaking in

Australia. 'We've got all departments covered,' they said. 'I don't even think they'll come close to us, to be honest.'

Well, we did stand a chance, as it turned out, winning the urn back in the Fourth Test at Trent Bridge. I ended up castling Nathan Lyon for the final wicket – quite a moment to cap my first summer as an England player. There's a photo of Jos and me celebrating that wicket which I have up in my house.

JOS BUTTLER: *Yeah, I've got that 2015 photo, too. That was pretty cool.*

MARK WOOD: *Because you were keeping for a lot of my career, especially in ODIs, you're always first on the scene with a hug.*

BUTTLER: *It's that moment when someone is celebrating and you run at them. I remember you being like five steps away and we made eye contact and you just know the biggest bear hug ever is coming. Then everyone else piles in and it's just a mass of bodies and yelling in your ears. Nothing beats it.*

The best thing about that was the game was over by about midday on Saturday, giving us an entire weekend to lap it up.

There was a speaker system in the dressing room, which we could all plug our phones into. Throughout the afternoon (and night), someone would cue up that video of Watson and Smith saying what they said, then someone else would follow it up with the clip of Zach Galifianakis (best known as Alan from *The Hangover*) doing a wheezing laugh from his film *Dinner for Shmucks*. We must have played that 150 times that night. I can still hear it now: 'I don't even think they'll come close to us.' Beautiful.

★

It's important to celebrate the small wins in day-to-day life, too. Got a new job? Treat yourself. Splash out on something nice. Just maybe don't do as I did and get talked into throwing money at something you don't actually want.

I was seventeen when I got my first contract with Durham. It was a deal worth £150 a month. Not much at all, but when you're seventeen and getting money, I felt like I'd made it. Getting paid to play cricket? Ha-way, off to Toon we go.

Me and my best mates from school, Scott Dunn, Jonny Storey and Glen Taylor, went into Newcastle to go shopping and splash the cash. We went into a few fancy shops and I came across this Armani shirt. They all persuaded us that it was worth the £90 on the price tag, so I bought it with little hesitation and strolled out feeling like a Premier League footballer.

I think I wore it once. It was blue with white trim, and short sleeves. You know in the hotel where you've got them blokes who just work the service lifts? Aye, one of them, minus the little hats.

JONNY STOREY: *I think to this day it is still the worst shirt I've ever seen. He wasn't even making that much money. When he was getting changed into it, me, Glen and Dunny decided we'd big it up no matter what. He walked out and we were like 'Oh mate, you look amazing', 'You'll regret it for the rest of your life if you don't buy that shirt', 'Treat yourself!'*

You learn your lessons, don't you? The main one here being to never trust your friends, especially if you think you can hear them scheming while you're buttoning up in a changing room. I was a lot more measured when I got my England call-up. It was exciting, as you can imagine. But there were nerves as well.

I was in Dubai with Durham during the 2015 pre-season, watching the airport conveyor go around and waiting for my suitcase. James Whitaker, the national selector, rang me up. It was an unknown number so I didn't answer it at first. He'd left me a voicemail and I rang him back and he said, 'Congratulations, you've been selected for the West Indies.'

It was off the back of a Lions tour. I hadn't taken any wickets but had bowled really well. I'd shown a bit of heart on some tough pitches. The coaches knew because they were smiling when I got off the phone and turned around and said congratulations. My dad was the first person I called: I remember him saying the hard work starts now, mind.

Turning up to an England squad for the first time is a bit like your first day at a new school. Liam Plunkett was going to be there, so I had one friend, and I had been on a pace-bowling camp with James Anderson and Stuart Broad, so I kind of knew them. But I was also thinking, 'Wow, I get to meet Alastair Cook!'

I didn't end up playing a game but it was an incredible experience. The perks alone were pretty special. Ah wow, you fly business class now! You get a suit! It's class! The next step is a national contract where you get a car and a phone contract, too. Back then, when data and roaming charges were a killer, it was mint.

Generally, how it works when you get selected by England, the team manager gets in touch, sending you an itinerary of where you need to be, asking what size you are for kit. When I got my England suit and tried it on, I took loads of photos. The badge, the tie. It was almost like I was putting on my country's battle armour. My mam was proud as punch, saying I looked so smart. And I'd just met my now-wife, Sarah, so I milked that – she was loving it as well. Great timing, it was.

Thanks to Sarah, there have been more big life moments to celebrate. Our engagement, our marriage, the birth of our son, Harry. I quite literally couldn't have done any of that stuff without her. I'd like to think she couldn't have done all that without me, too, particularly Harry. We work well as a team, as evidenced by the day after our engagement party.

We'd organized a do in our back garden and hired a big marquee, which was really lovely, and it meant we didn't have people messing up the house with their shoes or not using coasters. The kind of thing us cool cats worry about. The weather was perfect and it was a great occasion with close friends and family.

The following morning, Sarah decided she was going to take it all down herself like a superstar. I was in bed alone for about thirty minutes and I get this call on my phone. It's her.

'There's a gale force wind! This tent [it was a marquee] is going to blow over, take out the fence and damage our house and all the other houses!' I charged down the stairs in me dressing gown, get outside and see Sarah clinging onto one of the poles for dear life.

To this day I don't know why, but we decided the best thing to do was to get it on its side. I lifted out one of the pegs and, as I do that, an extra gust of wind picked both me and Sarah up and shunted us towards the house.

We had to call the fire brigade, who turned up lights blazing, getting everyone on the street out of their houses, with me and Sarah both in dressing gowns, clinging to the side of this tent for dear life. They came in, pulled one cord and the whole thing collapsed.

Luckily, they found it funny. Hilarious, even. I don't know much about fire safety protocol, but I'm sure they didn't have to take so many photos of us as they did. We're probably still plastered over the Northumberland County Council noticeboards as calls to avoid.

We fared better at our wedding, mind. You're not going to find a better go-to guy than me at weddings, especially when it comes to speeches. I've given four in total: three as best man and one as the groom. Given it's something a lot of people struggle with, here are some tips I've picked up along the way.

MARK WOOD'S GUIDE TO WEDDING SPEECHES

Best Man

1) Speak slower than you think

2) Sections are your friend. Break it down: an introduction, a bit about the bridesmaids and the bride looking lovely, but always make sure to big up your side. If you're a best man, have a bit taking the mickey out the groom, but round it out with a nice little story. Doubly important if he's likely to be your best man and you're going first. You don't need to give them another reason to dig a little deeper for skeletons in your closet.

3) Sip a drink after your first laugh. Savour it. It may be the only one you get.

4) Make everyone feel welcome. A lot of people won't really know each other. It can be quite awkward. At my wedding, I went for the following:

> 'It's great to have so many people here from Australia, South Africa, the Caribbean. People mixing from north and south. It's amazing how weddings bring everyone together. We've even got Labour mixing with Tories. Looking at you, Chef, on table seven [Alastair Cook is obviously a staunch Tory]. So that's table seven, comrades. Table seven.'

Nothing brings people together like a common enemy.

5) Weddings can also be uncertain times. Embrace it, especially if it's a big mix of different people from different parts of your life. Everyone is there for you and they'll do their best to mix for you. Like when Glen and Stokesy went to the bar for drinks and Stokesy bought a round for everyone, which cost £200. I can still see Glen's face when Stokesy turned around and said, 'Go on then – your round next'.

6) Always rehearse. Whenever I've written a best-man speech, I've tried it on my dad first. Though make sure you find someone patient and generous with their laughs as it can be a bit grating. By the third or fourth reading, my dad's not laughing and I'm worrying it's rubbish. You don't need that.

7) A grandstand finish. Now, this is the most ambitious of the lot and it might not be for you. But if you're up for it, try and finish with a flourish. Ideally something like an in-joke or a shared memory that you can go big on. For my best-man speech at Dunny's wedding, I went big.

When we were kids, me and him used to dance around to Status Quo. Now, Status Quo had a brown-haired one and a blond-haired one, so I would wear a brown tea towel and Dunny would wear a mustardy-white coloured one. We'd then play air guitar on tennis rackets to complete the look.

I mentioned this early on in the speech, turning to Dunny to ask if he remembered. He said yes, sheepishly, and I moved on to the next story. When it came to the toast, I pulled the cord:

'Well, for one more time, Dunny, let's make sure we're rocking all over the world.'

Cue Jonny Storey playing 'Rocking All Over the World' on the speakers – absolute banger, by the way – as I pulled two tea towels and tennis rackets from behind the curtain and we did it all again, one last time.

★

One thing you learn as you go through a life in the spotlight is that there's nothing better than celebrating with loved ones. The way I see it, every time I play for my country, I get to treat mam and dad.

The way they brought me up and the places they were able to take me to, the things they did for me, to return some of that by giving them a chance to be spoiled doesn't happen often enough.

Whenever you play for England you get tickets for the VIP box with all the other families. My parents love it: my mam is always grateful, talking about how good the food and drink is. I think that's pretty special. I still regret that they weren't at Trent Bridge when I took that winning Ashes wicket.

When I was new to international cricket, I wanted all my family and friends to experience it. However, that can become a great test of where your priorities lie, because you only get so many tickets. Sometimes you can get it wrong. Or rather, sometimes the people you invite can get it wrong.

For my first Test at Lord's against New Zealand in May 2015, Sean 'Sheep' McCafferty was there from Ashington. I got Martin Guptill edging to Cook at first slip and there were big celebrations from my family and friends in the corner he was in. By all accounts, they were going big.

However, my bleeding foot wasn't behind the line, was it? When the wicket was eventually disallowed as a no-ball, all the New Zealand fans in their area gave it straight back to them. They started having a go at me, shouting 'NO BALL' for every ball I bowled after, not realizing it was my people around them. At the end of that day I caught up with them all and it turned out Sheep nearly got into a fight! You'd think with a nickname like that he'd get on with Kiwis.

SEAN 'SHEEP' MCCAFFERTY: *In my defence, I didn't realize at the time there was quite a large New Zealand contingent around us. And worse still, because of where our tickets were, they were almost certainly friends and family of the New Zealand team. There were a few words exchanged there and I had to remember I was at the Home of Cricket and be a bit respectful. It might have kicked off if we were at Chester-le-Street.*

MARK WOOD: *You can't take us Ashington lads anywhere.*

I don't think anything will beat the World Cup final at Lord's for that shared experience when the game was eventually won.

After running around on the outfield with the team like a smiling headless chicken (you know what I mean) and giving it big when we first got back to the dressing room, I went back out into the crowd to fetch my family and friends in attendance.

By now, the stands had merged and were just one big blob. Everyone wanted to get on the pitch, and I found myself at the front of this huge mass of people in a strange situation where everyone's congratulating us but I'm also having to bat people away to find my nearest and dearest. It was like a scene from the *Hunger Games*, deciding who would get to make the trip into the inner sanctum. I'm not going to lie, I felt very powerful.

Eventually, I managed to get my parents, my auntie and uncle, my mother-in-law, my agent and my best friends out from the crowd and into the Long Room where the other families were. I could tell Storey had been crying. Glen and Dunny had already gone home because they said they didn't want to bother me! Can you imagine? They'd never worried about that before! Take this example from the final Test of the 2015 Ashes at The Oval when I got them all into the changing rooms.

I left them to it and was chatting to a few of the other guys, and some of the Aussies too. Suddenly, Rooty taps me on the shoulder and goes, 'Woody, do you know those guys?'

I turn around and Dunny is going through Joe's bag, putting all his kit on! And I mean ALL of it: pads, helmet, gloves, even waving his bat around.

A few minutes later, they're wrestling Cook – Sir Alastair Cook, as he's known these days – trying to get him into the showers, saying, 'Come on, mate, we've had a hard day, let's have a wash.' Imagine that: my first ever Ashes, my first ever series win, and one of my best mates is trying to drag England's greatest runscorer, fully clothed, into a shower!

JONNY STOREY: *There were a couple of moments when I thought, 'Hmmm, do we need to dial this down a little bit?' I think that was when Dunny asked Rooty for throw-downs while wearing his kit. Fair play to Rooty, after getting over the initial shock, he started chucking a tennis ball at him.*

SCOTT DUNN: *I'd probably say the moment it hit me was when I was getting messages back home from mates because they'd seen me on TV standing on the England balcony, holding the glass urn that was filled with whisky in one hand, and the tiny real urn in the other. I think that was also when the security were a bit concerned.*

STOREY: *Or when we were sat in the ice baths with Stokesy, all having a cigar. Dunny was spraying these bottles of champagne around – expensive bottles, too.*

GLEN TAYLOR: *We would never get them experiences if it wasn't for Woody so we were buzzing to be there with him.*

STOREY: *I felt like we were a bit out of place because we're a bit livelier. But Dunny kept saying, 'When will we ever do this again? Just take it in and enjoy it!'*

It's all part of a big lesson: however much these things mean to you, they mean just as much to those around you, the people who are so proud of what you are doing on their behalf. For them to share your success is great because you feel like you owe it all to them at moments like these. The people that always believed in you, even when you didn't. The people that got you through the hard times you never thought you could get through.

I've still got programmes from the World Cup final. I've even got the light-blue pads I got run out with. Thankfully, all the mud and dust from that rubbish dive I put in at the end was washed off by all the beer and champagne flying around.

I also took the World Cup trophy to Ashington. It's where I was made and, while it's not a big place, it's now produced three World Cup winners: 1966 football heroes Bobby and Jack Charlton, and me.

The trophy came up in a big box and only I was allowed to touch it. Which is just as well because, I mean, I know what this place is like: there was every chance it wouldn't have been returned to the ECB offices. Imagine that on the news? 'World Cup goes missing in Ashington!' I think I posed for a thousand photos while holding the trophy. I had arms like Arnold Schwarzenegger by the end.

I thought back to playing in 'World Cup' and 'Ashes Tests' in the garden with my dad, or with my mates on the street or at the side of the pitch at the cricket club. To see these kids turning up and seeing me with something that big and meaningful was surreal. Just writing those words gives me a shiver up the spine.

During the World Cup, I got every match shirt I wore signed by all the players. Because of it being a World Cup in England, I knew it was going to be special, so I wanted to remember it for the future with these mementos. But I also wanted to show my gratitude to those that supported me, so I gifted them to various people.

I gave one to the England physio, Ben Langley. He was there when I first started with the England Lions. I had a lot of ankle problems and he is a key reason why I'm playing for my country to this day.

I gave one to the ECB fast bowling coach, Kevin Shine. He spent so many hours with me behind closed doors and got me in a good place with my technique, always believing in me.

I gave one to Stevie Williams, my Ashington coach. He invested so much in me at an early age when he wouldn't have known how things would end up. He would work all kinds of shifts then turn up to the cricket club and coach all the kids, as well as play. He's the kind of selfless person who has influenced so many people, not just as cricketers.

I gave one to my mam and dad and another to my auntie who was with them at the final. One to the cricket club too, of course.

I thought what effect it would have had on me as a child to see a shirt up in the bar worn by someone from my club that had done something like that. Harmy's shirts were always up and really gave us a lift that someone like us was out there doing great things.

I grew up fifty yards down the road from the club. My family played there, my dad still helps set up the nets, and it was the first place I associate not just with cricket but all my loved ones. To be there as a World Cup winner, there in this small town. To think of the influence this will have inspiring kids from my little corner of the world. That someone might bowl and pretend to be me. Me? Imagine it! It was very humbling.

I never thought I'd get there. I still don't believe it. I'm just a normal lad, and I've won the World Cup. It's what you play for and it's also what you should cherish. Because, really, it's not just you that's won it.

As for the shirt I wore for the final – it's hanging up in my son's room.

2

HOW TO KILL TIME

There's no easy way to say this, but the imaginary horse is dead. On 17 July 2018, he was put down with an imaginary shotgun behind some imaginary curtains. I pulled the imaginary trigger.

He lived one hell of an imaginary life, full of real love and genuine popularity ever since he came into the world at Chester-le-Street, the home of Durham County Cricket Club. But by the end, he got pretty annoying. Not full of himself, like. It's just he became a bigger deal than me. Which was a bit annoying because he was imaginary.

He was born during a County Championship match for Durham. I couldn't tell you which one but boredom was getting the best of us in the field, clearly. Now, I obviously think cricket is the best thing in the world, but it does have its moments when it's also the most tedious thing in the world. Such as in four-day games when it's chilly and nothing is really happening.

Bowling? All over that. That's kind of my thing. I think I'm pretty mint at that. Even batting: I wouldn't say I'm the best at that. It's hard to say I am when I've not scored a century for England or Durham in eleven years as a professional cricketer. But I grew up as more of a batter and can still block or swing at a few deliveries when required. But fielding – no one enjoys fielding. The quality of fielding is incredible at the minute, especially with England. We've got some of the best in the world in our side, some proper freaks. But the enjoyment – or lack of – has remained the same for most of us mere mortals.

It doesn't matter what level you play, fielding when you're not bowling can be a real buzzkill. There's nothing worse when you're playing on a pitch that gives you nothing as a bowler, whether in Tests or ODIs. You can't just sack it off or wave the white flag, you just have to keep running in. Keep believing, even when believing is foolish. It's thankless work for the benefit of someone else – usually the opposition batters. Imagine doing your taxes for someone else? Like that. No offence to the accountants out there. Particularly mine.

In those moments, like on that day in Durham, you have to make your own entertainment for your own sake. Or, as me and Mark Stoneman did, your own imaginary horses. It started out with taking them for walks in the outfield where they weren't as close to the action and out of harm's way, feeding them apples (mine loved Granny Smiths). Then once they got a bit older – about four overs older – we used them to joust. Don't worry, RSPCA, if you're reading this – no imaginary horses were harmed in the making of this nonsense.

Technically, mine was a pit pony. Gorgeous fella, loved a trot and a graze. He started getting more confident and jousting with anyone and everyone. He didn't seem to like my Durham teammate Gordon Muchall and would constantly pick him out for jousting, which was a shame because Muchall is a great lad. In 2015, the *Guardian*'s Ali Martin cottoned on and asked us about him (the pony, not Muchall), and from there the rest was history.

That year saw me and the pony make our international debuts at the start of the summer. At the end of that summer when England won the Ashes, he put on a fancy little trot to pay tribute to wor teammates who'd done brilliantly to reclaim the urn off Australia. Unfortunately, that was the start of the untimely end to our relationship.

It wasn't his fault. Fame affects us in different ways, and when every fan who came up to me would only want to talk about the pony, it was only natural he'd get too big for his hooves. But honestly, it got so annoying. Every pub, bar, ground and even out in the street, someone would come up to me and ask:

'*Woody!* Woody! Where's your horse?'

'*Woody!* Can I meet the horse?!'

'*Woody!* Do a gallop for us, will ya?!'

I wasn't a late-night entertainer about to do an impression of a horse (sorry, pit pony) across a bar. Maybe I should have been more grateful for the attention. I don't really get recognized, even as an international sportsman.

Maybe if I'm with Joe Root (one of the best England batters of all time), Jimmy Anderson (legend, handsome), Stuart Broad (all those things as well as being tall and blond), Ben Stokes or Jonny Bairstow (both ginger). But you know, I've played Tests, one-dayers and Twenty20s for my country. I've won an Ashes and a World Cup and bowl quick. At least ask me to bowl a bouncer at a barman instead of neigh, you know? Even if they'd both be pretty weird requests, mind.

The pony's final day was a one-day international at Headingley. I don't tend to get a good reception there for some reason, but just when I thought they were warming to me, turns out they wanted to see the little guy. I'd had enough: I mimicked taking out a shotgun and put one right between his imaginary eyes. He'd had a good life, and it's maybe not how he thought it would end. But it's what I would have wanted.

DANIEL GRANT: *When we used to open the batting together at Ashington, he was very much the serious one. In fact, he was probably the most serious guy on the park, which is funny when you see what he was like early on in his England career with that bloody horse.*

JONNY STOREY: *He used to say he hated that. And I was like, well stop bringing it out! You're the one that brings it out. You're the one that leads it around the pitch pretending you're walking it. It's on you, not anybody else.*

He was talking about how he wanted to put the horse away for a while. I don't know if he thought because of it people weren't taking him seriously. People don't really lead a horse around in Test cricket, do they? There was that game where he takes this catch in unbelievable pressure, and then rides the horse around the boundary. I thought, ah no man. I text him that night, saying I thought you wanted to get rid of the horse. He's only got himself to blame.

MARK WOOD: *It was probably because I was trying to keep the crowd happy. But my loyalty to the horse had gone.*

Cricket is such a mental game, full of worrying and waiting, that you need little things like a pit pony to get you through sometimes. You can never take your place in the game for granted. Batters can score a hundred in one innings and get a duck in the next. As a bowler, your deal with the devil is that you can bowl brilliant and take no wickets and then bowl rubbish and take plenty. Even the very best feel like they've had more of the former than the latter. So you need to do whatever you can to keep your spirits up.

★

I never expected to play for England. I didn't even expect to play for Durham, to be honest. I wanted to play for my local side, Ashington Cricket Club, and didn't really have any ideas beyond that, growing up. The more you step up a level, the more you have to give: you've got to dedicate yourself to it, sacrifice time with loved ones and also your mind and body. And I've definitely given a lot of my body to cricket. If I didn't play it, I'd probably wake up every day in a lot less pain, though definitely a lot less happy.

Over the course of my career, I've had to do a lot of killing time: rehabbing for injuries (how long have you got? Plenty of time, presumably, if you're reading this), on long tours and in biosecure bubbles. I suppose it's the one thing everyone has in common – coping mechanisms to get you through the day, whether that's reading, meditation, hobbies or impersonating livestock.

Fielding is a bit like commuting, I suppose. Boring but a necessity. We can't listen to music on the field – how mint would that be, though? – but you do end up playing little games that make it more bearable, like how some people imagine they are Formula One cars when they're walking, commentating to themselves as they pass others on the street. Everyone has their own little quirks.

For example, when the batter drops the ball around the wicket and goes for a quick run, the best way to get the ball onto the stumps for a run-out when you're a bowler carrying on in your follow-through is to kick it. Because of the short time you have, reaching down to pick it up and then throw can cost you valuable seconds. And given most cricketers fancy themselves as footballers, it's a pretty common sight.

I can't tell you why, or when it started, but whenever I'm

in that position, I yell out the name of a famous Newcastle United footballer. Sometimes it's *'Shearer!'*, *'Asprilla!'* or *'Ketsbaia!'* (the Georgian striker who is best known for kicking seven shades out of an advertising hoarding after he scored a last-minute winner against Bolton Wanderers in 1998). If I get one on my left foot it's *'Ginola!'* I've not done an *'Albert!'* yet, though I'd probably have to dink one onto the bails in homage to his glorious chip against Manchester United.

I should say, I am not a Newcastle fan – I actually support AFC Wimbledon. The reason for that is blue is my favourite colour and when I got a Premier League sticker book when I was younger, I realized my dad looked like their goalkeeper Hans Segers.

I used to go to their games when I could, and even went to see them play at St James' Park decked out in the full kit when they played Newcastle. The rest of the family were pretty tense throughout as we were in the home end but me mam even managed to call Dean Holdsworth over for a photo. I got to meet a few more of the squad when they were training at Gosworth when I was six. Vinnie Jones took me into this room to sign autographs and speak to a few of the players. And I know what you're thinking – why don't I shout the names of Wimbledon greats when I try and kick down the stumps? Well, it doesn't quite work yelling *'Jones!'* or *'Holdsworth!'* or *'Leonhardsen!'* in a Geordie accent.

SCOTT DUNN: *Right, so this really annoys me. Woody must have come to fifty Sunderland games with me and yet he's always going on about Newcastle. I think he was asked on a Durham podcast if he preferred Sunderland or Newcastle and he said Newcastle! Can you believe that?*

MARK WOOD: *That's because the lad who was recording the podcast was a Newcastle fan and I did it as a favour. The Durham dressing room is full of Sunderland fans and so I thought I'd help him out. When we won the World Cup, Newcastle actually invited me and Stokesy to St James' Park. Sunderland didn't!*

To be honest, I'm going to have to park the kicking thing for a bit after I caught one a little too sweetly during the England v South Africa match at the 2021 T20 World Cup. I ended up lashing it past the stumps and the keeper and away for runs. Eoin Morgan was not happy.

In my defence, I've hit more than I've missed. I did mention cricketers fancy themselves as footballers, but I was actually all right, you know. I was on the books at Newcastle United before being let go at fourteen. I was a combative midfielder with a decent touch and pass, with both feet.

GLEN TAYLOR: *He was the captain of Bedlington Juniors, the team we both played for. He was this little chipmunk, this little meerkat – a tiny little, skinny little bony thing.*

But technically he was unbelievable. However, he used to wear the worst football boots as well. A-Lines they were called. He used to pride himself on the kangaroo leather that they were, while the rest of the team had the latest Adidas Predators.

MARK WOOD: *Don't listen to Glen. A-Lines are the best boots ever, hands down. Gianfranco Zola used to wear them, and it showed. I reckon the kangaroo leather put an extra spring in your step. And it was great that nobody else had them. I was unique. Be a shepherd, not a sheep.*

Being good at football came in pretty handy when I started playing for England because we used to warm up with games of football. They were always hard fought and intense: plenty of arguments over teams, disagreements on the pitch and a few other incidents. There were some big injuries too, enough that management have now stopped us playing it altogether. I was perfectly behaved, though.

JOS BUTTLER: *Are you going to tell them about when you took me out?*

MARK WOOD: *When? Oh…*

BUTTLER: *I remember it so vividly. It was during the 2015 Ashes. Obviously, I'm the best player, so Woody has come through the back of me.*

WOOD: *No, it wasn't that deliberate. The ball had come to his feet and I tried to nick it in front of him. Because he's got legs like a lumberjack, I couldn't get the ball so I ended up going through his calf. I looked at him and those bright blue eyes were full of rage. 'What the HELL are you doing?!'*

BUTTLER: *I had proper red mist. I thought, 'Woody's a football man, he knows what he's doing – he's tried to leave one on me.' I was spewing at you for a while. For the next ten minutes, I was looking for an excuse to boot you back.*

See? Tense.

★

Growing up, my parents used sport as a way to burn my excess energy. It was football in the winter and cricket in the summer, with some tennis and swimming among that. I was always out playing as a kid, whether that was in the garden of Mam and Dad's, my grandad's place or in the garages behind the back of our houses. That was a great spot for cricket, though you had to be careful with your shots. Anything on the leg side was fine, but anything hit on the up on the off side and you were asking for trouble. As with every neighbourhood, that was where this one miserable bloke lived. If you hit the ball into his garden, you wouldn't get it back.

I'm going to sound like an old man now, but it felt like growing up we spent every free moment we had outside. Sometimes not even sport: we used to play this game called Hares and Hounds. One group are the hares, who run off first. Then the 'hounds' have to chase them down.

Sometimes, we were running away from danger. Opposite Mam and Dad's was this housing estate that was dead rough when we were growing up. Every now and again we'd have to leg it to get away from a few of the lads who just wanted to make trouble for the sake of it.

DANIEL GRANT: *Yeah, there was a lot of that. As long as you were faster than the slowest person you were with, you were all right. It was survival of the fittest. Saying that, Woody was one of those people that the people you'd leg it from would just be like 'Oh, you all right, Woody, how are you doing?' It's like he had diplomatic immunity.*

What can I say, I'm a people person. I was friends with all the charvas (or chavs, if you're from down south). I say 'charvas' affectionately because they were always good to us because I was good at sport.

Cricket meant I had a good throwing arm and so when it snowed, they'd come to me to nail targets they had picked out. Like I was a seasonal hitman. I knew they were right by me because one time I threw a snowball into a group of girls and it missed them and hit a dinner lady.

She was in so much pain and the teachers caught wind of it. But the charvas didn't grass on us and they all took the blame together. I think it was against their mafia code.

Football was my main sport growing up, but I probably spent more time playing cricket, whether at school or at the cricket club and all the time in between. I don't think there was a day that went by in the summer when we weren't playing cricket. GCSE revision, the six-week summer holiday: we'd net every single day. Somebody always had a key for the club gates, which we'd hide to keep for ourselves because we weren't supposed to have one. Every day we'd walk up with wor cricket kit to the club and be there all day. Our parents weren't worried – other than how we'd pass exams if we weren't studying – because they knew exactly where we'd be.

JONNY STOREY: *Honestly, those were the days. We'd mess around with the bowling machine, face it at 95 mph. You couldn't do that now, like, for health and safety reasons. I remember that time we had it on one side of the boundary and shot balls in the air for high catches. The first one was on close to 100 mph – it shot over the other side of the ground, into the houses. We heard a crash and ran over and quickly dismantled the bowling machine to get rid of the evidence.*

MARK WOOD: *It was Geoff Prudhoe's house – he was the chairman at the time! It set the alarm off.*

As we got into our teens, we started going out more. Like all lads, drink became a thing. Not for me, but that ended up meaning I was usually the designated driver, especially as I passed my test first, which I didn't mind all that much. Considering how much my mates liked to put away, even from a young age, it's impressive that only two people have thrown up in my car – Jonny and Sheep. Jonny is the outright leader on that front: one for trying to pull the steering wheel of the car to get us to pull over so he could spew on the side of the road, and two for trying to wind my window down to throw up out of as we were on the move. Let's just say he didn't quite get it all the way down.

My first car was this red Corsa. Beautiful little thing with a spirited engine. It tried, god bless it. We used to drive around in it at night just taking in the sights. We weren't even really going anywhere, just literally driving around Ashington and Morpeth, the neighbouring town, where I live now, just spending hours people-watching.

Ashington in particular is a funny place where you'd see things you wouldn't see anywhere else. We'd go around the pubs and back lanes, just looking for obscure things like urban David Attenboroughs. And usually we'd find them. We once saw one of our mates from school having a fight in one of the back streets at like 11 p.m. There were a couple of lads scrapping, one doing a lot better than the other. Eventually, one got off the floor and we were like, 'Hang on – is that Nelson?' We called him over and asked what he was doing: 'Ah, I was just fighting with this lad – I was doing him over!' You absolutely were not – you were on the floor!

I still remember when we found what we thought was a dead body lying across a wall in Lynemouth. I drove up to it slowly, first flashing my headlights, then beeping my horn. This bloke was totally unmoved. We wound down the windows and asked if he was all right, and after getting no response, we thought the worst. Then Jonny Storey got out of the car and was shouting at him to get his attention. Still nothing... until he got face-to-face and the bloke suddenly woke up and started screaming. Jonny nearly had a heart attack. Thankfully, the bloke was just mortal (incredibly drunk).

JONNY 'SATAN' STOREY: *We also used to shout at people out the window. Woody was the worst. He used to just shout 'Hoogedy boogedy!' at passers-by. When he was driving, he didn't want you to do it so, of course, that just made us do it more.*

GLEN TAYLOR: *Even now when we go out, he'll just be randomly making ridiculous noises while we're walking along the street. In public! It's like Woody, what are you doing? You're not driving around Ashington any more – you're an England cricketer. Everyone knows who you are, and you're going on like this. Pull it back a bit, even I'm feeling embarrassed.*

STOREY: *I still remember that one bloke we shouted at who was so startled he dropped his shopping. We got to the traffic lights and looked back and this bloke was chasing us with what was left of his carrier bags.*

MARK WOOD: *I mean, it was an easy car to spot. But yeah, I was terrified. He didn't pick his shopping up, he just started running up to the car. All the lads in the car were like, 'Woody, he's getting closer – what if he kicks your car?' Then I was thinking, you're right, this is a brand-new car and Dad will kill us if it got any marks on it. I ended up driving through a red light just to get away.*

I suppose we should explain Jonny's 'Satan' nickname. I mean, it explains itself, really. I think a teacher gave it him because he was always getting into trouble, which just meant he was a lot of fun to be around. That's still the case. We were taken to a pub once when we were thirteen after a game and the coaches ordered thirteen Cokes for the kids and three pints for themselves. All of a sudden, they realized one of the pints had gone missing. Jonny had taken it and drained it already. Next round, he did the same. He was a right wrong-un when he was a kid. But he's come full circle – he's now a policeman.

We weren't trouble. We never went out of our way to annoy people. We were just all incredibly silly, enjoying being young and enjoying hanging around with each other. I wouldn't change a thing about any of our time together growing up. Except maybe the colour of that Corsa.

★

All sporting dressing rooms claim to be the most unusual. But I can't think there are many that beat the dynamics of a cricket dressing room. When you think about the amount of time we spend in them, especially for four- and five-day matches, and on tour, it's really quite unique. People have their favourite spots to sit and each ground's rooms have their own characteristics. No matter the size, they can be vast or constricting, clean or messy, boisterous or quiet.

The more you play at a certain level, the more you establish a preferred spot around people on a similar wavelength. You get used to the people around you, their quirks, what they like and what they don't. And, of course, their bad habits. It's not so much a clique, you just end up in your own little ecosystems within an ecosystem.

I'll be honest, I think a lot of my teammates over the years will feel like they've drawn the short straw when they're sat next to me. I'm quite fidgety, especially on the morning of games. I'll be singing, talking lots, just full of nerves and excitement, properly revved up. For players who have quieter routines, I imagine I'm not the best neighbour. Especially in dressing rooms where there isn't much space, like in the Caribbean.

CHRIS WOAKES: *I think my favourite example of this was the first morning of the St Lucia Test in 2019.*

MARK WOOD: *With Broady?*

WOAKES: *[Laughs] Yes! You were doing your usual thing: clicking your fingers to the song being played on the dressing-room speakers, talking crap, dancing around. Meanwhile Stuart Broad is sat there right up against you, collecting his thoughts, drawing on all that experience to focus his mind. Or trying to, at least. I was sat opposite and I could see him slowly getting to breaking point. Then he snapped.*

WOOD: *It was like being back at school – 'Woody! If you want to sit here, tone it down, son!' He then mimicked turning down a dial.*

WOAKES: *Did you move in the end?*

WOOD: *Nah, I reined myself in. I just made sure to go to your side when I wanted to mess about.*

JONNY BAIRSTOW: *That's when I try and get around you. Because I know it's nerves and I know you need someone to mess about with. You're a big kid that likes to joke around and have a few pranks. But you've got such a kind heart because you want to do so well for everyone and please everyone, so I know it comes from a good place.*

Rain delays are always interesting. If you play cricket long enough you become a pretty good judge of how long rain clouds set in for. In the England dressing room we've got more radar and satellite info than the Russians. Every day we get presented with a sheet of the day's forecast, which is generally pretty spot on and you can pretty much plan your movements around it.

Sometimes a quick shower will mean you're only off for twenty or thirty minutes. The longer ones, however, which you get a few of in England, take a lot of getting used to and you need to get creative. Because we are not allowed to have our phones because of anti-corruption betting laws, you've got to go pretty old school. None of this scrolling on Instagram or TikTok.

Some people sleep. Others play card games. Some lads will play dressing-room cricket: no attacking shots, just defending, with fielders around the bat and you can be out one-hand one-bounce. Sometimes there's a dartboard knocking about. Some go off and get a coffee or read a newspaper. If you know it's going to be a big delay, you might also go to the indoor centre to have a net.

I flit in between all that, depending on my mood. I don't like to sit still. I'll generally be the first one to go, 'Anyone, cards?' I get bored if I'm not doing something. I have to expend my energy into other things. I talk to people, mess around.

It was established early on in my cricketing career that I was a bit of a menace during these breaks. I remember being fourteen playing in the Ashington second XI. There was this senior player, Stuart Tiffin, who was a coach that really helped me early on. He used to do his kit immaculate: his bag was packed perfectly, tops ironed and folded.

We were playing cards in the dressing room while it was raining and I won one hand and ran around this tiny room to celebrate, just to rub it in. I was still wearing my muddy spikes and stood straight on the middle of Stuart's open bag, right on his folded, washed, pristine whites. As my foot's made contact, I just felt this arm hit me in the back of the neck. 'I'LL KILL YA!' I can still hear the collar of my shirt ripping as I got away. He'd still have hold of me today if it hadn't.

Games are a big thing. There are a few boardgames knocking about but what we end up doing is far simpler:

- *Guess the Song*: a tune hummed, all very self-explanatory

- *Whistle-offs*: pretty much the same, although this extends to theme tunes. No one comes close to my rendition of *University Challenge*

- *ABC:* A Wood family staple, this. The aim is to start from the beginning of the alphabet and work your way through, writing down, say, names of boys if that's the category. When the time is up, you compare answers. If you have one no one else has, you get ten points. So the more obscure, the better. Occasionally, if you've got a ridiculous one, you can nab fifteen. My speciality is 'body parts'. I've had that many injuries, every obscure part of the body is stored away for this. The os trigonum – look it up, thank me later – nets me fifteen every time. I could probably do a round on ankles alone.

If games aren't your thing, then it's about finding someone you vibe with and just chilling out. Me and Jimmy often gravitate to one another and fire *Friends* quotes or puns at each other. Then he'll get out a crossword, and I can't help with that because I don't get any of them right so then he gets annoyed and I've got to move on. I've never dropped a catch off his bowling, but I'm sure it can't be as bad as giving him the wrong answer for seven across.

I don't mind organized fun, but there's nothing quite like just talking rubbish with a mate. So much of our lives, as sportspeople or otherwise, is measured in numbers and achievements. We tend to use those as measures of whether we've had a good time of it or done something well. Those moments, however, when there's nowt to do and it's just you and someone you get on with, can be the most enjoyable. We'll all retire with our records and our averages and our accomplishments written down. But those days when we're just winding each other up, or in a bar chatting about all sorts, are the moments you'll actually miss. Those quieter moments away from the spotlight, often behind closed doors like a dressing room, are the ones that are more personable and more cherished. I certainly enjoy those more than watching the cricket. I hate watching the cricket…

If you don't want to know the score, look away now

A lot of us remember where we were during that miraculous 2019 World Cup final chase. Around 30,000 people were at the ground, chewing through their fingernails. Millions more were doing the same at home. Many of you would have been crowded around a TV or radio at your cricket club or found an Irish pub on holiday that was showing it. But for an hour of England's first fifty-over World Cup final in twenty-five years, as Ben Stokes and Jos Buttler were rebuilding our innings with a 110-run partnership for what would be the most dramatic win in English cricket history, I was in a darkened room sat on a washing machine.

'Are you… going to move?' asks the dressing-room attendant who was just trying to do his job and wash the towels to ensure we had a fresh supply.

'I can't, mate.'

'But… I've got to chuck these in and get them dry by the end of the day,' he says, carrying a big basket of laundry.

'You don't understand, mate. I've got to stay here. We're winning.'

'Can I at least switch it on while you're sat on it?'

'Go for it. Honestly, mate – if I move now and one of these two get out, it'll be all on me.' On it goes, whirring into its usual turns and jumps while I'm perched on top, trying to pull myself together.

'Why aren't you watching it from the balcony?'

'It's a long story,' I say as the drum starts to whirl underneath me, knowing he's not got the time for it. Well, now I can explain myself.

One of the biggest cricket superstitions passed on through generations but which makes absolutely no sense is that when your team is batting and things are going well, you can't move from your position. It doesn't matter where you are: sat down in the changing room, on the balcony, pitch-side in one of those dugouts or even on the toilet – more common than you'd think – you simply must stay put to avoid the jinx. Similarly, if things are not going well, you have to move. Because wherever you are is not helping. I don't make the rules, that's just the way it is.

Batters who are in next tend to always be watching the match live to see what the bowlers are doing, how the pitch is behaving and what-not. Us bowlers, however, generally take it easy. Yet I am an incredibly nervous watcher. I can't watch anything live because I'm too much of a wreck, fearing something bad is going to happen. I get told off for making other people anxious.

The last 2021/22 Australia tour, by the way, was the first time I thought to take in the first ball of the series.

It was my first Ashes tour, something I'd been looking forward to since forever. I was 'with' the squad in 2017/18 but didn't get on the park. So I thought I'd walk up to the upper concourse we had access to and take in the atmosphere of the Gabba, which is an incredible venue. Then, yep, Rory Burns gets bowled off that very first ball. I went back downstairs and didn't watch another ball again. If you're reading this, Rory – sorry, that one's on me.

I've established my usual watching spots in most grounds by now. At Lord's, it's perched on one of the beds in front of the TV in this physio room down the corridor about halfway between ours and the away dressing room. The delay in the pictures means I hear the cheers first. So I'll usually get a warning if something good or bad has happened by the muffled noises coming through, and then turn to watch what has occurred.

This is where I am when Jason Roy and Jonny Bairstow are strolling out to chase down New Zealand's 241. We were confident because we felt it was a very gettable total. I believed in them enough to change into my comfy training top and pants to settle in and watch us bring it home. That, right there, is bad cricket karma.

Hand on heart, I just didn't think I would be needed. Yes, I thought they had too many, but I backed our lads. We'd done brilliantly for most of the World Cup. Just as I was getting settled, J-Roy gets out (28 for 1), then Rooty (59 for 2). So begins the quest for a World Cup-winning spot.

Turns out the other bed was just as cursed. Bluey (Bairstow) gets out, and now we're 71 for 3 chasing 242. I'm done with both beds by the twentieth over. Now I'm on my feet and I can't stand still. Worst thing of all, the floor has square panels. So now I'm in this room, pacing, watching the screen and also making sure I don't step on any cracks. I'm doing the same sequence as well, back and forth, over and over, as I know it's a safe path.

By now, I've got company. Phil Neale, the team operations manager, came in after the third wicket and sat in the saddle of one of the warm-up bikes. We end up having an argument because my walking is doing his head in and his pedalling is winding me up. 'You've got to calm down, Woody,' he says, just as our captain Eoin Morgan gets out (86 for 4). Fuck it, that room is dead to me.

I decide to head to the changing room because I know there is a back area near the toilets that has a small TV. But I can't bring myself to watch anything. It's also slowly dawning on me that I might have to bat. I hover in the corridor between the toilets and the changing room, lost in this smelly No Man's Land. While I'm here there's a big noise from the crowd. Usually I can tell if it's a boundary or a wicket but my senses are all off now. Thankfully, it's a four from Stokesy. I now have to stay.

The only problem is there is no place to sit. Just a washing machine, and as things are going well, I know what I need to do. Have I found the right spot? Finally? I think so. Jos and Stokesy are taking the partnership on. I'm not comfortable, literally or figuratively, but things are better than they were half an hour ago.

It's at this point the dressing-room attendant walks in, looking to do his job while I'm in the way. I shift my legs over so he can open the machine and put in the detergent. Before he closes the door he looks at me like he has opened the curtains one morning and is wondering why I'm stood in his garden. On goes the machine.

So here are two of the best white-ball batters in the world out there turning around a final, and I'm bobbing up and down on a machine that this lad has set to 'fast spin wash'. The attendant ended up staying, as did another, and their chat helped calm my nerves as the runs were picking up. But I couldn't really offer anything because the vibrations meant I was talking l-i-k-e t-h-i-s t-h-e w-h-o-l-e t-i-m-e. 'S-H-O-T S-T-O-K-E-S-Y!' 'C-O-M-E O-N J-O-O-O-O-O-S!'

Even with the vibrations jolting my senses, I can tell we are doing well. The cheers sound like our fans, and the more often they come the more confident I get. Suddenly, there's one I can't make out. The delay from live to the TV means I'm watching it as Jos carves a slower ball out to deep extra cover where Tim Southee takes a blinder of a catch (196 for 5). 'Why, Jos?!' I think to myself. 'Why take him on? Just keep playing.' Now I think we're going to lose. It's done. No chance.

Jos felt that too. I had started to get ready when Jos came into the dressing room, a bed in the middle of the room in his sights. He starts going to town on it, punching this table, shouting, 'You stupid idiot!' and 'Why the hell did you do that?!' He's never usually like that. He's a fierce competitor but at the same time he's not someone who reacts badly when he gets out. He's usually quiet and keeps to himself. But he was punching the bed, throwing his pads on the floor, then hitting the physio bed with his pad and, finally, dropping to his haunches, staring at the floor, swearing. He looked up at me and the whites of his eyes were now dead red. Have you ever seen *The Mask*? You know, when Jim Carrey goes all loopy when he puts the mask on? Like that. But, you know, Jos.

I was really shocked by it. I was thinking, 'Oh hell, like, he's gan wild here. He's never like this.' I imagine he was looking at me and thinking, 'Why is this clown padding up when he's batting eleven and there are four others in before him?' By the time Woakesy gets out (203 for 6), I've got my kit on, pads and eveything. I didn't want to feel rushed. I even had my helmet on, like a tit.

It was only then, as I decided to go and watch the action live, that I noticed Rooty lying on the couch that was facing into the dressing room, with its back to the game. Every now and again he would look over the top to see what was going on and slink back down. It was like he was playing Cowboys and Indians and he was peering around for any enemies. Except, everyone was an enemy and they were getting closer.

Usually when he gets out he's disappointed but he sits up, watches the play, encourages all the other lads, talking to the batters going in about what the pitch and the bowlers are like. Not here, though. He's in his own world, hiding behind a couch, slowly losing it like the rest of us.

The only person who is up for chatting is Rash (Adil Rashid). We just look at each other and we've got this telepathic conversation going on. By the look on his face I know he's thinking, 'We're going to have to bat.' And my look screams, 'Geez, I know.' Nothing needed to be said.

I've never spewed through nerves but I was so close in that dressing room, in this posh little marble basin we have in the changing room. Massively over the top but it looks absolutely top drawer. Gold taps and that. And I was on the verge of redecorating it.

I started thinking about what I'd do. Lockie Ferguson was finished so it would be Jimmy Neesham and Trent Boult. Boult tends to bowl yorkers or slower cutters into the wicket, so think about hitting hard down the ground. Neesham, similar. So I've got two lengths to deal with so I start practising shots in the dressing room, trying to make people think I know what I'm doing. But I was shitting me pants.

I can talk you through every ball of that last over to Stokesy. The first is a yorker that he jabs to cover. The second he hits quite hard to cover. Both dots. Fifteen off four needed. We've lost.

Then when Stokesy hits that six, we're all just shouting without celebrating. Come on, Stokesy. One more. Then he plinks that two and he slides in and the ball hits his bat... oh my god.

The gentlemanly thing to do is not cheer. But when we saw that ball going for four, everyone is jumping out of their seats. As the ball hits the sponge, the whole dressing room goes nuts. There's dried fruit flying everywhere. Bats and shirts laid out for us to sign are being tossed around. People are gan ballistic. We knew we shouldn't be cheering. But what else do you do?

With three needed off two balls, Rash gets run out coming back for a second. No one said anything to me before I left the dressing room because they were glued to the replay of Rash's run-out and I had bolted out of there with everything on. Apparently, someone in there turned around and thought I'd gone missing and checked the toilets to see if I was having an *8 Mile* moment and throwing up before going out there.

I was getting slapped on the back in the Long Room as I sprinted through and out onto the field. I had actually injured my side at the end of the New Zealand innings but that was in the back of my mind. I was haring on like a madman. I was only about halfway through my charge out to the pitch, when I saw it was two needed off the final ball, that I realized I was wearing my chest guard, arm guard and massive thigh pad. Why am I wearing these? I'm not on strike, I just need to run. Why have I weighed myself down with all this?

JOS BUTTLER: *I can look back on it now and laugh, but you're right, Woody. I was watching you walk out with one ball to go, needing to run a two, wondering why the hell you were out there in a full coat of armour...*

When I got to Stokesy, I just said, 'I'm going to run, mate'. He looked back at me and he had these glazed eyes. Just so in the zone. I don't think he heard or cared about what I said.

Weirdly, the thing in the back of my mind when Boult was running in was the Mankad. I was thinking about making sure I wasn't out of my ground when he gets in his delivery stride in case he runs me out and we lose. Maybe I could have got a quicker start if I ignored it? Would he really run me out at the non-striker's end in a World Cup final?

Stokesy hits the ball to the leg side and I'm just saying in my head, *Tap your bat in at the top end – do not be one short!* I've hammered it down at that end so we've got the tie, and I turn and head back to the other end and put in what might be one of the worst dives in living memory. You know when you teach kids to dive into the swimming pool when they're little? 'Put your chin on your chest and just fall in' and they end up belly-flopping? Exactly like that.

I knew I was well short but I jumped head first towards the line. The knee flap of my pad got stuck in the ground, which meant the Velcro part of my thigh pad got stuck in the dirt too and ripped off. I think I was gone by a furlong.

That image of my dive, I think I received that about a hundred times from my mates over the next month. Laying into me, asking why I was so slow, why I was wearing all that gear. One friend told me milk turns quicker than I do.

There I was, face down in the dirt. Super Over on the cards. I looked up and could tell no one really knew what was going on. I get up to my feet and turn to chat to Stokesy but he's something like thirty yards away because he decided to boot his bat further than he hit that last ball.

My side is completely knackered, by the way. I properly can't breathe now. Whatever's left is hanging by a thread. I catch up with Stokesy and he looks shattered. Absolutely shattered.

It was a phenomenal effort from him already. And even then, with the match still to be decided, I was so proud of him. Here was a guy I grew up with: played against him when I was at Northumberland and he was playing for Cumbria, seen him lead by example in the academy, lead by example for Durham, and now here he was leading by example for England. I also felt sorry for him, that he put all that effort in. It was impossible at one point and, somehow, we were still alive. I can't imagine he remembers what I said, but I put my arm around his head and pulled him into my shoulder and was hammering into him that we were all there because of him. 'You kept us in this game. Now we're going to win it.' I've got that photo in my house.

By the time we got to the dressing room, it was more of a state than when I left it. Everyone was scrambled, buzzing because we were still in it and nervous because we didn't really know what to make of the Super Over. Reserve umpire Aleem Dar was in there, explaining it all because nobody knew what was the craic with it. Morgy and Trev are talking to Aleem, and then I pop up in front of Aleem and tell him I can't field because my side is knackered. It was the least of his concerns.

The other lads in the changing room were all over the place. Jase couldn't find his box so I had to give him my own. We're talking among ourselves about who it's going to be to face the Super Over. Morgy asks Stokesy, who is sat a few seats away from me. He's empty, but says yes.

By now, Jos has calmed down. When he starts doing his heel-flicks – a warm-up where he flicks his heels to his bum while jogging on the spot – you know he is ready to go. Totally different to an hour ago when he was going wild like Jack Nicholson in *The Shining*. I looked at his corner and everything was so neat and tidy: all his bats were lined up, spare gloves arranged neatly. He's some kind of wizard – I still don't know how he cleaned up so quickly when all that chaos was going on out there. But that said to me that he was in the right frame of mind.

Given I'm basically useless at this point, I was going around asking if anyone needed anything. When Jofra gets asked if he wants to bowl the Super Over, I was ready to reassure him and talk through plans with him. But he just shrugged his shoulders and went, 'Yeah, fine.' And I thought, oh right, you are fine. You've got this.

Then all of a sudden, someone asks where Stokesy is. There's a bit of commotion because they don't know where he is. But a few of us knew he'd nipped out to the back bathroom for a cigarette.

I really envy that. Not smoking, but the ability to just take himself away from all the madness and have a moment to himself.

To this day, I'm amazed no one saw him. The way the home dressing room at Lord's is, if you were to be in the outside bit of the Tavern Pub, and looked straight up at where the changing room is, you can see into the shower room. The glass is frosted but obviously he'd opened the window so you'd have been able to see in. Imagine someone walking by after watching that, maybe to rush to the bathroom or something, and looking up: 'That's Ben Stokes, isn't it? Tab on, in his full batting kit? Well batted, Stokesy! What is that, a Marlboro? Yep, good brand that, pal.' Crazy.

I decided to watch the Super Overs from the bench outside with the reserve players. The washing machine had served me well, but this needed something different altogether. After Stokesy and Jos did the business, Jofra had sixteen runs to defend. I was absolutely bricking it even though I knew he was the right man for the job. He'd only been an England cricketer for the last few months, but he'd been a superstar for years. I knew he could handle the responsibility. It's just I couldn't handle the pressure of watching him.

You'll hear a lot of sportspeople say watching is harder than playing because you get used to being able to influence what happens on the field. I think maybe that's why we have all that superstition and emphasis on where we sit and what we do when we're not involved. It's our way of contributing, or at least fooling ourselves into contributing. And the more I think about it, maybe that's OK.

So many of us go through life wanting to be involved in something more, something greater. I'm lucky that sport and cricket allows me to feel that. People joke that cricket is the most selfish of the team sports because concentrating on yourself and putting in a brilliant personal performance benefits the team. But in moments like that, when your turn is gone, you're all bound together. That even when your own go has come and gone, you might be able to appease the universe and the cricketing gods for the benefit of those out there in the middle. I'm sure all the ridiculousness going on in our dressing room was being replicated across that corridor in New Zealand's.

Of course, not all cricketers are nervy sorts. Some, like Moeen Ali, are just too chilled. I'll never meet anyone as cool as Mo, and nothing sums that up more than that Super Over Jofra bowled. When Jimmy Neesham hit him for that six, the whole ground gasped, apart from the few New Zealand fans dotted around the stands. All of us are silent until Mo, sat with us, goes: 'Maybe don't bowl this one into the middle of his bat, Jof.' Cracking jokes at a time like that?

Before the last ball goes out to Jase for the run-out, after he's misfielded one and thrown to the wrong end for another, Mo goes: 'He's going to bowl a leg-stump yorker here... As long as it doesn't go to J-Roy we'll be OK.' He's got the best sense of humour, Mo. As with his batting, his timing is perfect to take the pressure or awkwardness out of any situation. He made that whole last over bearable. Thankfully, he was only half right on that last ball.

It all happened in slow-motion. When J-Roy picks up and the throw comes in and Jos has gone in front of the stumps, I think I'm already out of my seat because we were basically right behind the ball. By the time he takes the stumps out I'm leaping over the advertising board. It's taken six different lucky spots but, heck, we've only gan and won the World Cup!

3

HOW TO BE FAST

R icky Ponting is looking at us. I know this because I checked to see if anyone was behind me. I've been burned like that before. Now he's walking towards us and, I'll be honest, I'm a little scared.

For a generation of England cricketers and fans, Ponting and his Australia were the boogeymen. They won everything, smashed everyone and particularly enjoyed beating us. Yes, by the end of his career, we managed to give him a bit back with Ashes wins in 2005, 2009 and 2010/11 when he was captain. But even now the sight of him sends shivers down my spine. Especially as he's getting closer.

What does he want? The team are warming up before the start of the second Ashes Test in December 2021, and I'm trying to think if I've annoyed him. Did I slag him off in an interview? Unlikely. Maybe I tweeted something back in the day about him? Nah, definitely not. The year 2021 was when the ECB got on us to sort out our Twitter feeds after Ollie Robinson got done at Lord's in the First Test that summer. The only tweet I was worried about was slagging off some builders who took the mickey out of us when they caught me singing in my car on the motorway.

Oh no, now he's right in front of me. If he hits us, do I hit him back? We're in the middle of the Adelaide Oval here, so it's not like he's not got back-up if it does kick off. Not that he'd need the help.

'Why the hell aren't you playing?!'

'Ermm. OK. Hello, Mr Ricky Pointing,' I replied, like I was back at school and he was a teacher who'd caught me skiving. 'We think the pink ball might move, and they're resting me for the next game.' He didn't seem to buy that excuse.

'I can't believe you're not playing!'

'Yeah, you know,' I said, before mumbling something about how we've got an attack that'll take twenty wickets or something.

He shrugged and moved on while I just stood there, a bit shocked. I couldn't believe it. I just had a conversation with Ricky Ponting. THE Ricky Ponting. A guy whose name is up in bright lights given how much he's seen and done in international cricket. And he thinks I should be playing.

Later that day, I rang up my mate Dunny. 'Can you believe this – Ricky Ponting was telling me I should be playing?!'

I used to write his name in wor book and now he's there, telling me he thinks I'm a good bowler. Mad! The 'book' in question was a textbook. When we were kids, Dunny and I and a few others would play cricket or football in the garden or out on the streets and pretend we were playing big cricket or football matches for England. I would also write match reports, transfer news, rumours, stuff like that. All made up. A lot of the time we'd make up the names of players too, but when it came to England v Australia (cricket) or England v Germany (football), we'd get the proper players in there. And Ponting was one of them. His pull shot, his toughness – I was just in awe of him as a kid.

SCOTT DUNN: *It's crazy. The players we used to do bowling impressions of and bat like, all those people you idolize when you're younger, they are the ones praising you for the press. There are a lot of people who give you credit or slag you off. But there are some people you think, 'If he's said something, I need to take his word for it.' And I reckon for me Ponting's up there in the top three for that!*

You only realize just how good you are at something when someone else notices. I don't know if this is a fact of life, but I definitely think there's something to that. Even when you put the work in day and night to be as good as you can be at it, you never really know how you stack up. And I say that as someone in a sport in which we're all ranked in some way.

When Ponting came up to tell me I should have been playing, we were standing in one of the best grounds in world cricket – after Chester-le-Street, of course – in an

Ashes series. Obviously by that stage, I knew I was all right. You don't just get on an Ashes tour through luck. It wasn't like I boarded the wrong flight at Heathrow. I know I had bowled quick in that First Test and was causing Aussie batters difficulty, including getting Steve Smith out for 12, which was a big deal considering he averaged 65 against us going into that series. We'd worked on a plan with Jon Lewis, our bowling coach, of having a 'straighter' field, with maybe even having more fielders on the leg side rather than the off side, which isn't conventional. But he's not a conventional batter. Basically, it meant when he was blocking it from off stump, he's not just getting off strike into mid-on, midwicket or square leg. You're still attacking the outside edge. So, he was not going anywhere and I managed to deliver the ball I wanted, which held its line a little bit and took an edge through to Jos behind the stumps. That was particularly pleasing – something we had talked about and worked on that came off.

Even so, my instinctive reaction to Ponting saying I should have been playing was of doubt. What, me?

That's certainly how I felt throughout most of my cricket career – and life, really – when people would praise us for something. Perhaps that's because of my upbringing. My parents raised me to be respectful and not take anything for granted and I've tried to stick with that as much as possible. Be as genuine as possible and be down to earth.

Don't let things, good or bad, get to your head. Always strive to be better.

Plus, the world is a big place. English cricket is a big place. You never know who is out there doing what you are doing better than you. I feel like each step up has been a steady realization of what I can do. I'd never believed I would play for England. I never believed I'd even play for Durham, really.

DEREK WOOD *(father): We only ever envisaged he'd play local cricket. Mark played for fun. He was that kind of kid: he just loved being outside and being with his mates. There are strong local leagues here and a lot of local leagues have played here. I played against Courtney Walsh, Ian Bishop and Desmond Haynes. The standard is competitive and, to be honest, we never thought he'd play outside of that sort of environment.*

MARK WOOD: *When I was a kid, we used to watch the Ashington first team intently. They'd be the ones you would emulate and look up to. They won the league one year and us kids ran onto the field and gave them a guard of honour. We aspired to be playing with them, really.*

★

The first time I realized I was quick was playing for Ashington Under-18s against a local club, Tynemouth. I had just got back to the top of my run-up when Jonny Storey ran up to me with the ball and, in his typical way, informed me the batter I was bowling to was finding it difficult to negotiate the speed at which I was bowling, and the late movement I was getting through the air and off the pitch. I mean, that's what I assumed he meant when he shouted, 'Woody, this lad is *bricking* it!' He's scared? Of me?

I was fifteen at the time and I'd never been particularly quick, or even really a bowler. I grew up as an opening batter who was a bit of a swing bowler. I was a small lad and was constantly reminded of that. I played for our second XI from the age of twelve, so always saw myself as a kid among grown-ups.

'Woody, honestly,' said Jonny. 'You are bowling fast!'

As he went back to his position, I stood at the top of my mark and looked around the field. And things were just... different. The wicketkeeper was a little further back. Our lads were a bit more vocal in the field. It was still early in the match and we were doing OK, so the enthusiasm was understandable. But they seemed a bit louder.

One of those leading the chat was Jonny. He was always the main one sledging on my behalf. Not because I gave him that role but because he couldn't help himself. We'd always have a chat between balls. This time though, he looked wired, in short on the leg side, saying all sorts to this kid who was preparing to face the next ball.

'Really? Me?' I bowled him the bouncer Jonny wanted and he gloved it in the air to second slip. We went wild.

JONNY STOREY: *You bowled that first ball and Granty the wicketkeeper took it above his head, and I remember thinking, 'Wow! Where's that come from?' You did it again, just from bowling full, and I had to run down and said, 'Mate, bounce him!' There was a kid who came out at number six and I'm still convinced he stood on his stumps because he couldn't hack it.*

Another time came a couple of winters later. Around the age of sixteen, I had been brought into the Durham academy and was working with their coach, John Windows. It was just a usual session I'd do: working on my action, how I was running in at the crease. After a couple of full run-throughs he just casually came out with an observation.

'You'll be able to bowl 90 mph.'

'What, me?' Again, I thought he was talking rubbish. 'Nah.'

Later that year, Ashington played a game against Chester-le-Street Cricket Club. I was batting and one of the local players started calling me 'Pac man' because I was chewing up balls.

Now, in club cricket where I'm from, all the big dogs would sledge a little bit. This bloke was nothing at all, really, but any time they would pipe up, he would jump on the back of it. You know like when the big bullies at school do something and there'd always be some little no-mark who could never handle himself, jumping in, trying to be part of it? He was that lad. I was starting to get really sick of it.

Later in the match, he walked in to bat and, fired up, I bowled the speed of light. I got him out within three balls: bounced him, bowled it full, short again and he nicked off to the wicketkeeper. During the celebrations and the huddle after, my teammates were in bits and the look on their faces was priceless. 'Honestly, Woody... that was *rapid*.'

By then, it had twigged. Yeah, me.

★

To this day, I can't tell you why I bowl fast. According to various records, I've bowled some of England's quickest deliveries and spells in red- and white-ball cricket. But I couldn't tell you how. I know my deliveries skip off the pitch quicker than others who lose a bit more pace after the ball bounces; I run hard into the crease and give my all. I've got a braced front leg, which means when I smash it down on the crease, there is no bend in my knee so I go over the top of it, like when you're on a bicycle and put on the front brakes. My back hip fires through quickly, which allows a big delay in my bowling arm so it comes through like a slingshot. All the force goes from my legs, up through my body, up to my shoulder.

But I've nae got the muscles like other fast bowlers. I've got noodle arms and I'm not exactly tall. Maybe five foot ten on a good day. I feel guilty taking the extra legroom seats on planes that are reserved for the fast bowlers when we travel. Well, not that guilty.

Maybe I developed a better understanding of what I'm doing. My Ashington coach Stevie Williams honed my technique early. John Windows, Neil Killeen and Alan Walker fine-tuned it when I started working under them at Durham from 2008. From there, Kevin Shine at the ECB, along with other England bowling coaches like Ottis Gibson, Chris Silverwood and Jon Lewis have helped me fine-tune my action.

I think a lot of people around me would say they didn't think I would make it as far as I have. My inner circle, like my dad, never thought I'd play for England. It didn't happen overnight, but it wasn't exactly something people assumed or even predicted would happen.

DEREK WOOD: *It was when he started playing for Durham that I realized he might have something a bit extra special. That, actually, he's better than I thought. There was one particular game when Durham played Australia A. Angela and I turned up after work, and we can't have been there longer than a few minutes and he took four wickets, which included Australian internationals like Peter Forrest and George Bailey. He was nearly unplay-*

able. That was the one time I thought, 'Ooooh hello – what do we have here?'

STEVIE WILLIAMS: *He was a late developer. He went through some tough times physique-wise, really: he wasn't really average height as a boy and into his early teens. He was lean, he didn't quite have that build. He was always borderline at Durham. He'd often ring me and we'd have a chat about what he should do, if he should go somewhere else. I had contacts at Northamptonshire at the time and that was an option.*

DANIEL GRANT: *He always had that x-factor. That unmentionable thing that exceptional people have that you don't have, and you can see it's there but don't know what it is. That's how I'd describe it. So did I know he'd make it? No, because it was hard to say he was in the top one per cent of the one per cent who actually make it all the way to the top. But he did seem to have something other people didn't growing up.*

WILLIAMS: *I do remember he started to get quicker when I was playing with him in the second team. He was still a batter, mind, but he was also coming into his own as a thinking cricketer. One weekend, I had to work a Saturday shift so I made Woody captain at fifteen. There were some raised eyebrows from the senior players at the time. Why is this kid getting that gig? He responded by opening the batting and scoring a hundred. He was unphased by it all.*

SCOTT DUNN: *There was a bit of Joe Root about him as a batter. Obviously to a different extent, but everything was very prim and proper, technically correct, everything under his eyes. He was always batting in higher teams for his age and doing well. Though I still remember those seven ducks in a row he got when he first came into the first team.*

MARK WOOD: *It was six!*

DUNN: *Nope, definitely seven. I still remember him walking around to the other side of the ground when he walked off to just sit and mope in silence. He got dropped to the seconds the next week, scored seventy-odd, came back up and never looked back. Now he comes out for England and he's loose as hell! He's a far better batter than what he shows, though I suppose batting nine or ten, what chance have you got, really?*

What I can say is that bowling fast changes everything around you. Batters have less time to react and are more prone to playing at balls they shouldn't. You've also got that fear factor other bowlers don't have. You can hurt people, which isn't a great thing to be proud of, but it definitely comes into the equation with short-pitch bowling, where you can target the body for dismissals. That intimidation factor upsets rhythm and knocks them out of their comfort zone. I got Shimron Hetmyer out in a Test match at St Lucia in 2019. The way Hetmyer played it, he didn't move his feet and just jabbed at the ball. From my point of view, it looked like he instinctively flicked out with his hands at the ball. You know, like when one of your mates shouts, 'Think fast' and chucks something at you as you turn around? Like that. It flew to Rooty at first slip who was quite far back.

In the last Ashes Test of the 2021/22 series in Hobart, I got Usman Khawaja out with a bouncer that almost took his head off. That night, I got back to the hotel and shared a lift up to my room with Justin Langer, the Australia coach at the time. He smiled at me and said, 'Woah, that bouncer was a brute, wasn't it?'

Even when a batter does win a battle against you, in the back of their mind they're thinking about what you might do for revenge. At Trent Bridge in 2015, I made the foolish decision of hitting Mitchell Johnson over extra cover. He was bowling at about 95 mph at the time and was fired up after they had been bowled out for 60 on day one when Broady took that eight for 15. I remember my satisfaction of nailing him for four immediately turned to dread because I knew I'd angered the bloke who had torn us to shreds in the previous series in 2013/14. His comment of 'You're dead, mate!' as I held the pose to admire the shot confirmed that. The next ball, I was watching his hand and, before I'd even moved, it had hit the keeper's gloves behind me. I didn't see it.

Now that Johnson has retired, I can probably get away with telling the story of when I hit him for six in 2017. It was a game for the England Lions against Western Australia at the Optus Stadium in Perth. He bowled a length ball and I smacked it down the ground for six. I thought the next ball was going to be at my face, so I backed away and got bowled and he just laughed at us as I was walking off. I had to act all disappointed inside as I went back to the dressing room, but internally I was thinking, 'Oh my god, I don't even care – can you imagine, I've just launched Mitchell Johnson over his head.'

The mark it left on my bat was a beauty. Right in the middle of the middle. I used to admire it at training and tell anyone that would listen about it. Anyway, later that winter, we were in New Zealand and Danny Reuben, the media manager, comes into the changing room during a training day in a bit of a panic. 'Ed Sheeran wants a bat!' Who does? Ed Sheeran. It turned out he was in New Zealand on tour and I think he wanted a bit of memorabilia as he's a cricket fan. Anyway, Danny has come up to us and asked us for one because he knows a batter won't give one up easily, even to a world-famous musician. So I said, fine, he can have this bat if he wants. But I want a guitar in return. Swapsies. Danny was like, 'Yeah, no problem.' Did I get it? No! I've given up this bat which hit Mitchell Johnson for six and got nothing in return. That bat should have been framed and mounted on a wall. And instead it's probably being used to knock around apples and oranges on Sheeran's tour bus. I'll never forgive Danny for that.

During the first innings of the Sydney Test in January 2022, I carted Pat Cummins for a few sixes. Three, to be exact – the most he had conceded in a Test innings. When I came out for the second innings, his fast ball cracked me in the ribs. I thought, 'OK, we're even.' Unfortunately, that was just the set-up for the next delivery, which was one of the best balls I've ever faced in my career. He smashed me toes off with an inswinging yorker and to this day they've still got a tinge of green to them.

It felt like an explosion had gone off in me foot. I was on the floor in agony. I honestly thought they'd have to cut my foot off because it must have been in bits. And while I'm giddy from the pain, I've got Bairstow in my face going, '*Review it! Review it!*' I hadn't even realized the umpire had given it out. Sorry, Bluey, I'm too busy wondering if I'll ever be able to walk again. By the time I did the 'T' with my hands to review it, Jonny had already done it because I was five seconds too late. As the screen loaded for the review, Jonny turns and goes, 'Are you all right?' Not really, mate!

JONNY BAIRSTOW: *I was trying to take his mind off the fact you were in a lot of pain. And even then your character was still coming out saying things like, 'Ooooof Jonny, he's blown my shin off!'. Yeah, sure he has – but you can still review it!*

It was very out. I'm hobbling off like a duck, humili-
ated, and all the Sydney crowd are quacking at me because
I'd gone for a two-ball duck. Humiliating. Aussies love
nothing more than embarrassing their opponents with
pace, and they have the best fast bowling attack in the
world as I write this.

When I was nineteen, a few of us Durham lads were
asked to bowl at the Australians for their net practice
when they were over for the 2009 Ashes. It's commonplace
to get local bowlers in as you don't want to tire out your
own, and it was a huge honour to be bowling at these
lads, some of the best around at the time. I was in a net
where Shane Watson was batting and he chins it, so you're
running in a bit scared. As a net bowler, you're there to
help, not make a name for yourself. Wait your turn, bowl
your balls, don't do anything daft and make sure the
batters get the best practice. Basically – do as your told
and keep your head down.

I was clearly making an impression on them because at
one point, Mike Hussey – Mr Cricket, an Aussie legend
– came to me and told me to bowl a short ball to Watto.
Well, if he's telling me to, I should. So I did. It whistled
past his head and Watto was surprised. He growled a
bit and chucked the ball back to me. Then Hussey came
back like the devil on my shoulder: 'Give him another!'
I wasn't sure. 'Nah, go on, mate, do it. He won't expect
another one!'

I decide to put my back into the next one and it's even quicker… and he absolutely smashes it. I mean, out of the middle of the middle of the bat. In fact, he's hit it so hard it's bounced off the net and back to him. He picks it up and chucks it back at us, with a few words: 'You idiot! How about I bowl at you then, champ? You're just a net hero. Keep laughing!' I definitely wasn't laughing then. I didn't know what to do, and turn to Hussey who is falling about in hysterics. Luckily Watto doesn't hold a grudge. He and I were briefly teammates at Chennai Super Kings and he couldn't have been nicer. I know what you're thinking. 'Woody – if Mike Hussey told you to jump off a bridge, would you do that as well?' And the answer is aye, probably. He's one of the best batters to have played the game and I'd be desperate to earn his respect.

Secretly, I loved that Hussey wanted me to bump Watto, because it was an aspect of fast bowling I really loved – everyone wants you on their side. You're like a special weapon that few teams have and everyone wants to use. Having that kind of pace in a team emboldens your teammates, as much at international level as it did when I was fifteen. That's quite a cool feeling. Like you have a super power and you can choose whether to use it for good or evil. With great pace comes great responsibility and all that craic.

I think my favourite use of this 'super power' was to settle a score for a teammate at Palm Beach Currumbin Cricket Club in Australia when I was twenty-two. We were playing First Grade (or first team) cricket out on the Gold Coast. Club cricket there is a bit different to here because they play over two Saturdays, each containing 75 overs. It takes a bit of getting used to and can be tough but the wins are very rewarding. It also means any ill-feeling from the first Saturday festers ahead of the next.

Anyway, we were batting first the first week, and Richard Burgess (Burjo to us) was playing a typically dogged innings. He must have scored 20 off about 40 overs. He didn't give his wicket away but didn't get any runs. The opposition were doing their bit to remind him of his strike rate, getting him angrier and angrier.

With them batting the following Saturday, he was ticking that week in training. He kept coming up, trying to fire me up: 'You're going to kill this bloke, aren't you?' I'd be there bowling to my mates and he'd sidle over and go, 'Yeah, you're just warming up, aren't you? That's why you're not bowling fast now, right? Yeah, I like that, mate. Real nice. Remember, you've got to kill him!' I was a hitman and Burjo was making sure my trigger was well oiled.

So, it comes to Saturday and Burjo's nemesis comes out to bat. While we're in this huddle, we realize there's one missing – Burjo, who is currently walking with the bloke out to the middle, having waited for him at the gate, telling him all sorts.

We set this leg-side field as if I'm going to bounce him. Burjo is the man out at deep square – the one in position to catch the ball if this guy decides to try and take me on. I bowl the first ball and this guy plays and misses, and Burjo sprints in from deep square, shouting, 'Yeah, let's see how you like it! Yeah, have it! Go on, Woody, knock his head off!' By the time I get to the bottom of my mark, I look up and Burjo is sprinting back to his position.

The next ball is a bouncer that flies past his nose. Burjo's back on the scene: 'Yeah! You get out here, mate, and I'll walk you off this field!' The next one I pitch up, nick, straight to third slip. We're all celebrating and, again, there's one fielder missing. True to his word, Burjo walked this guy from the wicket to the boundary rope, absolutely in his face: 'You weak man! You were sledging me and look at you – you're soft!' Had it been anyone else, I'd have probably advised Burjo not to carry on like that because he'd only be targeted more. But one thing I forgot to mention was that Burjo was an ex-rugby league player. No one was going to come back at him.

★

Now, I'm not a coach so it would be a bit reckless if I tried to teach you how to bowl fast. But what I can do is talk you through how it feels to bowl fast.

For this, you're going to need to shut your eyes and listen to me. Actually, no, don't do that. Open them to read this. Maybe shut your eyes if you've got the audiobook.

HOW IT FEELS TO BOWL FAST

Nondescript whale music plays in the background amid the throng of chatter in the stands. As your captain hands you the ball, the Barmy Army start singing your name.

Let's start by taking a deep breath. Breathe in... and out. And once more, in... and out... You are now standing at the top of your mark. The ball is in your hand. Feel its seam in your fingers. You are relaxed. You are calm. The Barmy Army are singing your song. Your body is fresh, shoulders loose, spirit high. You are playing for England at home, and you have never felt more in your element. This is where you've always wanted to be.

You look up and survey the field. Slips, a gully, point. Someone in short because, hey, you're a fast bowler. You're the one they all came to see. All the expectation is on you to do what you do. A bit of pressure? Sure. That's to be expected. After all, you do something not many others in the world do. Quite a lot of pressure when you put it like that. But don't worry. It's fine. You've got this.

Your eyes then fix on the batter. This is the battle – between you and them. The wicketkeeper, the fielders, the umpire, the crowd, your family and friends who have travelled all that way to see you, everyone else in the ground, the millions watching on television, judging you – they are all irrelevant in that moment. Don't worry about them.

So, this batter. They've probably been in for a bit. Maybe they've just come to the crease. All you know is that you hate them. Perhaps hate's a strong word. Or it isn't, because all they want to do is make you look bad. They'll want to hit you for a boundary and if they do, a slow-mo of the shot will follow on the big screen to embarrass you even more. A commentator will say you bowled too full, too short or too wide and pick apart your technique. Twitter will go into overdrive and say you're shite or something, and at the end of the day the captain will be asked in his press conference if you should be dropped for the next game. Later that week you'll be driving somewhere and switch on the radio and hear someone talking about how maybe you need to be rested because you can't play two games in a row. All because this useless batter hit you for four. Honestly, sod them.

Sorry, no – calm. That's it. Remember the breathing at the start. Do that again. Heck, you've probably done it five times already and are getting lightheaded as you eye up this scumbag before you finally set off. Quickly. None of this jog stuff. You have to charge to the crease, making sure you get there just when you reach your top speed. Don't think about it too much. You've done this since forever. This is how you got to this position: all the overs in county cricket and ten thousand times more in practice. Don't fret. Seriously – *stop fretting*!

It's a straightforward run-up, marked along the way by the notches you painted earlier that morning when you were going through this all in your head. It seemed a lot easier then, didn't it? The stands weren't as full, you were having a joke with your teammates. You might have even painted a smiley face at the top of your run-up along with your initials. This is fun, remember? Just a sport. With the wicketkeeper, the fielders, the umpire, the crowd, your family and friends who have travelled all that way to see you, everyone else in the ground, the millions watching on television, judging you. All irrelevant in that moment, of course.

As the crease gets bigger, your speed increases, while your stride remains consistent. Because as soon as you get in line with the standing umpire, a few feet away from the crease, you are going to need to leap into your gather. And as soon as you land on your right foot (left foot if you're bowling left-handed), you need to stomp your left foot down on the crease and send an incredible amount of force through it – seven times your bodyweight, in my case. On impact, you brace your landing knee and fling yourself over the top of it.

Internally, it's going to feel like you are the chain of an anchor that has just been dropped into the sea: all those connective links clicking into place one after the other. Each one needing to be in sync else you don't bowl fast enough, accurately enough – or you seriously hurt yourself. For fans of medieval weaponry, think of yourself as a human catapult. The run-up and gather are the cranks, pulleys and chains being set up. And as you land to deliver, everything from your shoulder down is rigid to fling yourself forward into a *whooosh!* In the moment you deliver, everything is silent. All the external noises are blocked out. As you come over that front leg, even the batter disappears from view and, for a split second, your mind is empty.

By now, ideally you've let go of the ball. If you haven't, you've got a problem. Even if you have, there's still the follow-through to negotiate. Refinding your feet isn't particularly easy, especially as you need to ensure you don't run over the 'danger zone' in the middle of the pitch, which is naturally where your momentum is taking you. If in doubt, do as I do and just fall over.

You pick yourself up and survey the end product. If you're lucky, it hasn't been hit for a boundary and your shame and career are safe. If you've got a wicket, why not go mental? Perhaps a section of the crowd have been giving you grief? Maybe even the batter? Feel free to rub it in their faces. If not, then get back to your mark. You've got five more to bowl to finish the over and five more overs to come after that. Not to mention the two other spells of all this you've got to get through before the day is over.

Oh, and don't forget those deep breaths.

★

So you're probably thinking, yeah, bowling quick sounds like an awful lot of hassle. But let me tell you, when you're in the zone, there's nothing like it. You can't feel the grass beneath your feet. Your legs feel light. You don't even really feel like you're sprinting. All you can feel is that build-up, build-up, build-up, build-up, build-up... and then WHOOSH! That release.

I felt like that on Finals Day at Edgbaston for Durham against Yorkshire in 2016. I was out of the England team and was coming back from injury on a big stage against England players. I got big wickets – Gary Ballance, Jonny Bairstow, Liam Plunkett, Tim Bresnan – and I bowled well at Rooty, all top players. It reinforces your self-belief like nothing else.

Similarly at the same ground, I bowled well against Australia in the 2017 Champions Trophy, with 4 for 36 off my ten overs. I got David Warner, Steve Smith, Glenn Maxwell. That was the first international tournament I felt like I belonged, and to get them players out, in a big game, felt good. I felt like the difference maker. Maxwell was the most satisfying. Eoin Morgan had asked us to 'bomb him' – bowl a load of short balls at him – and he swotted it to deep midwicket where Jason Roy was. Jase took the catch right on the boundary, close enough that they had to review it. He was a dangerous player, it was a brilliant catch and the plan had come off. If he hits that a tiny bit more, that's six and I'm under pressure.

The first time I felt like that in Test cricket was in St Lucia, where I picked up my first five-wicket haul. It was also the first time I ever felt like the fielders were irrelevant. I was bowling where I wanted, at pace, not thinking about my run-up, where I was landing on the crease or where they could hit it. It was the first time I felt like an England cricketer, not just a player who played for England.

It makes all the other bad spells worthwhile. The spells where you don't necessarily bowl badly, but you feel it more. Those times when you're walking back to your mark and your body is reminding you of the toll you've put on your bones and joints. You feel like you're sinking into the ground, through your legs. You ache. When you set off to go again, you still have that build-up, build-up, build-up, build-up… WHOOSH! But it's just not as fresh. It might not be as explosive when it's your third spell of a Test match day, but that's something I have got better at over the years.

I think that's the aspect of fast bowling that surprises a lot of people, including fast bowlers. The relentlessness of it. The expectation and responsibility of doing it three times a day, five days in a row, for years. It's why the guys at the top are adored by everyone else, especially other fast bowlers. My favourite at the moment has to be Cummins. I think he's immense, and not just because he owns half my foot. Just consistently fast as well as accurate and keeps turning out performances spell after spell, day after day, match after match. It's remarkable really.

Because every time you do it, it takes that little bit out of you. Bits you don't get back. You're never as fresh, you're never free from pain, never as explosive as the first time, whether in a day or even in your career.

But I suppose all the things that are worthwhile in life are earned. I'd love it if fast bowling came easier to me. I can't tell you how much I envy someone like Jofra Archer. Now that man is a Rolls–Royce of a fast bowler.

Throughout the 2019 World Cup we had a great partnership that bordered on a friendly rivalry. We'd gee each other up to bowl quick and it was so much fun.

He was convinced they never put his speeds up on the board, all this kind of stuff. But then mine would come up all the time and I'd get him to have a look. But whenever it was under 90, he'd shout, 'Oh, you just warming up?' So I'd be like, 'Right, I'll show you next, pal!' The next one might have been short, wide and a pile of rubbish – but it was never slow!

At the innings break of that World Cup final, our analyst came to me and told me I'd officially bowled the fastest ball of the World Cup at 95.7 mph. He also told me my 18 wickets were the second-highest of our team, but there was only one stat I cared about.

As soon as Jofra came through the door, I couldn't help myself.

'*Jofra!*' I shouted, desperate to tell him the news (and leave out that his 20 wickets were the most for our team). 'You'll never guess who got 95.7?' He looked at me and he was not impressed.

'Look,' I offered, 'you tried, mate. Keep your head up. It happens. Live and learn, eh? Maybe you'll get to 95.7 one day.'

He furrowed his brow and looked me up and down. I had ice packs on my ankle, knee and side. I was barely able to stand and grimacing in between smiles.

'Look at me,' he said, pointing down at his whole body, sleek, comfortable, barely a drop of sweat on him. 'And now look at you.'

I looked at myself, like an extra out of *Band of Brothers*, and thought, 'Yeah, fair enough. I've had to rip my body in half to get anywhere near you.'

Unfortunately, Jofra has endured his own tough times with injuries recently, which goes to show how tough fast bowling can be even for someone as smooth as him. I can't wait to bowl with him again.

★

St Lucia was a big moment for me. As I mentioned, it was the first time I felt like I belonged at Test level. I went on to do well in the 2019 World Cup, though had to miss that summer's Ashes through injury. I went on to take another five-for in South Africa at the start of 2020 and then career-best figures of 6 for 37 in the final Ashes Test in Hobart at the start of 2022. It was also the first time I felt fans and commentators were really into me. People were talking about how I should be playing. Not only Ponting, but Aussie pros like Brett Lee, who was an inspiration of mine, and the late Shane Warne, too.

Articles were being written about how I needed to play as much as possible, especially with the injuries to Jofra and Olly Stone, our other fast bowlers. It felt like there was a shift in the way people were appreciating me.

One of the biggest shocks of playing for England is the coverage because there is so much of it. Much more than when you're playing county cricket. I get it – it matters that much more. You're playing for your country on the biggest stage and so many people are invested in it.

All the papers, television and radio – they've got pages and air to fill. There are a lot of opinions and analysis around and naturally not all of it is going to be about how good you are.

I used to read everything but it became too much after a while. I had to step away from Twitter because I found myself always drawn to the bad stuff, all the criticism.

Even my mates used to wade into arguments. It didn't feel like a healthy thing to obsess over.

I still remember one journalist's comments during the 2017/18 Ashes. I was close to an appearance for the Perth Test, one of the quicker, bouncier surfaces in world cricket. This journalist didn't agree: 'Talk of Mark Wood is just ridiculous, as if a bowler with no match fitness and pace that has been exaggerated into something it is not, can come into the intensity of a Test match to bowl in 40-degree heat and create mayhem.' Fair to say those comments came in pretty handy as fuel to prove him and others like him very wrong.

People were always telling us what Sky commentators had said about me on air during play. At times it felt like being back at school: 'Have you heard what so-and-so is saying about you?' No, what's he been saying? Is it bad? Were they having a go? So I decided just to take myself away from it all. Get a bit of distance.

I was probably a bit stubborn at the beginning, wondering why all these people were commenting on us. I get it now, and accept it as part of the game. Some things still get on my nerves. Like when I get asked about other English fast bowlers, particularly Jofra. It feels like they're trying to stoke up a rivalry between us when there isn't one. I love bowling with him, he's one of the best we've got. But I always get the feeling people are waiting for me to say something they can misconstrue as a challenge or a dig at him, print it and then create a bit of controversy out of that.

That being said, I wouldn't be here today if I hadn't followed up on something someone had said about my run-up. It's fair to say not only did this guy know what he was talking about, but he also happened to be one of the greatest fast bowlers of all time...

MICHAEL HOLDING: *The first time I saw Woody, I thought to myself 'pace!' I love to see bowlers that give batsmen a little bit of trouble at night. Not just on the field, but they're going to bed and thinking, 'Oh god, I've got to face this man when I wake up!' So I gravitated towards Woody immediately.*

Because of my fast-bowling background, I thought he seemed to be hustling a bit into the crease, you know? Malcolm Marshall used to hustle into the crease but at no point did it look like he was rushing, like he wanted to get in a certain number of steps before he got there. I got that impression with Woody.

MARK WOOD: *You're analysed when you first get into the team and stuff like that, especially as it's the first time an audience and maybe even some media see you. Mikey was someone I had a huge amount of respect for and I heard him say that about my run-up.*

I decided to approach him that one morning at Lord's and just said, 'Look, can I speak to you about it?' I mean, I say that, I was a bit nervous at first. I actually didn't go up myself first. I asked a couple of backroom staff: 'Do you think Mikey would be all right if I asked him about what he said?' Ottis Gibson said, 'Oh, mate, of course, he's a great guy.'

HOLDING: *The thing is, I don't try and impose myself on anyone. Even the West Indian cricketers who I'd feel even more comfortable approaching, I don't because I don't want anybody to think I know it all. I would say things in commentary, and if anyone wants to approach me about something I said in commentary – fine. I am quite open and quite relaxed and quite happy to explain why I said it. Even if they don't necessarily agree.*

WOOD: *I didn't feel like you were imposing on us at all. It felt, if anything, because you were someone I look up to, you were giving your expertise on something that would actually benefit me. It wasn't a criticism, it was actually saying, 'Look, if he did this, I think he might improve.' It was constructive. You had something to make me better, and I wanted to tap into that.*

HOLDING: *As I explained to you, and to most fast bowlers, the run-up is used to build rhythm. And sure, some fast bowlers run in quicker than others. If you want to sprint and you think that you need a bit more time to use that sprint to get in, the only thing you can do is to lengthen that run-up. That is how you have to combine all the aspects of fast bowling. Of course, the less rushed, the more rhythmical you are, the more likelihood you are to be in full control of your body when you get to the crease so that everything goes where you want it to go and do less damage.*

WOOD: *I was probably a bit stubborn at the time. This run-up had taken me this far. Do I change it, do I not? It probably wasn't until my first operation that I thought, yeah, this run-up isn't working for me because there's too much pressure going through my ankle. I should have probably listened to him a bit earlier.*

The funny thing is, behind the scenes, coaches were secretly saying these things to me about my run-up, but not as plainly as Mikey. They were sort of saying, 'Oh, you look great with a longer run-up,' or 'Have you ever tried making that approach longer?' And I was just like, nah, nah, nah – no need.

The thing about speaking to Mikey, he wasn't just telling me what I wanted to hear. He said by having a longer run-up, it'd give me more momentum, more rhythm and explained everything. So I felt more at ease to make the change after that.

HOLDING: *I don't go around broadcasting this and that. But I feel good within myself that I contributed in some way to that.*

WOOD: *Well, when I got my second five-wicket haul – 5 for 46 in Johannesburg – you were waggling your finger at me going, 'I told you! I told you!'*

HOLDING: *[Laughs] Well, if I can help in any way and you benefit from what I say, I feel good about it! Because I want to see somebody like you, with that kind of pace, have a long career. Two or three years, even five years – almost anybody does that. When I see a fast bowler who comes along and can preserve his body and last towards a decade, I love that. And if I have any impact towards that, I love that.*

WOOD: *Well, thank you very much, Mikey. I wouldn't even have a book if it wasn't for your advice!*

Since I changed my run-up, I've played more games, bowled quicker and been able to sustain it. The more rhythm and momentum I've had has made it easier on my body in general. I should have listened to Mikey sooner.

It would have been easy to miss or dismiss Mikey's suggestion had I been so head down and insistent that all the external noise was not worth listening to. I mean, it would have been daft to think I know more than a West Indian legend.

But when you're trying to make your own way in the world and so focused on yourself, you can miss something that can make you better. It's worth bearing in mind that, whatever you do, you're never too good to listen. There are people in this world that come along and give you that one nugget that pushes you on that little bit further by telling you something you hadn't heard or they tell it to you in a way that cuts through. You just need to find your own Mikey.

JONNY STOREY: *I still remember when I came over a week after you'd played in a game on Sky when Holding was commentating on you. I walked into your front room and you were watching the match back and were rewinding the bit where he praises you. You were just replaying it over and over again.*

MARK WOOD: *That was Durham against Surrey in the Pro40 when I was just breaking through. It was one of the first TV games I played in. I actually got J-Roy out, but only after he carted us about. And then I got former Surrey batter Matt Spriegel out. Holding said, 'Well bowled' in that voice and I had that on record. Whenever anyone came around, I'd be like, listen to Michael Holding here: 'Well bowled!' I tried to get it as my ringtone.*

★

At the end of the Ashes tour, someone sent me a screenshot of a tweet from CricViz (a data analytics company) of the twenty fastest spells by an English bowler in Australia. I had eighteen of them, including the top ten, all from that one series. The other bloke, who was responsible for two of them, was Stephen Harmison. Not bad for a couple of lads from little old Ashington.

It was a nice little boost after what was frankly a dispiriting tour. As was the 6 for 37 at Hobart. I didn't think I bowled that well, to be honest. I'd definitely bowled better in the three Tests I played before that one, especially given how people were talking us up. Even the players, like Marnus Labuschagne and David Warner, who both smashed us that winter, were being really complimentary. That was nice to hear, if a bit weird.

I've never really been one to carry that stuff with me. If I bowl well one game, I'll feel confident going into the next. But in terms of comments and praise, it's nice at the time but it doesn't really give me a boost going forward.

Maybe that's a bit weird. A lot of people say arrogance is a necessity for playing professional sport. But I've always seen that as a negative. Confidence is good: in your ability and the team. Arrogance, by my definition, goes past that. You're too cocksure, too into yourself. You think you're better than other people.

Maybe some people need to think like that, and even if they do tend to be the most irritating members of a team, if it works for them, it works for the whole. I just don't see why you can't be the best you can be and also the best person. Of course, I hope at the end of my career people respect us and think, 'He was a good player, a good bowler.'

Above all else, I'd want them to think I was a good bloke. That I was good to play with, that I was great to have in the team, that I gave everything every time I played. I'd rather people saw us like that rather than 'good player, but what an arrogant bloke'. And, of course, that I was absolutely rapid!

4

HOW TO LOVE

'm standing at the bar at Ashington Cricket Club at the start of 2015. It's band night, one of many the club had on throughout the year. Back in the day, there used to be a regular disco here on a Sunday night and it would always be heaving. The kind of night where if you weren't there by 6 p.m., you didn't get in and you would have missed out on a belting night.

Not going to lie, I was in my element. I was on the radar of the England team and there was buzz about me as a quick bowler worth keeping your eye on. Life was good and I was feeling good. And then I saw her.

I'd seen her before. Long before. She only lived fifty yards around the corner from us. She went to the town's Catholic School (St Benet Biscop) and I went to the naughty boys' school (Ashington High). You know, Montague and Capulet stuff. Our paths would occasionally cross, with friends of friends, even the odd game of Hares and Hounds. I always thought she was a good-looking lass but we'd never crossed paths at the right time. That was until there was this do at the cricket club. She had just gone to Manchester for university and was back home.

We'd made eyes at each other all night, that kind of craic. She spent most of her time mingling or on the dance floor, while I was sat with my mates. My trip to the bar was well timed. Just as there was a bit of a lull, in between tunes. And sure enough, she was soon on her way over.

I decide to engage. A cutesy wave, that'll do it, I thought. Of course, before I do, she waves first. I'm buzzing, of course I am. But time to play it cool. Because you don't want to come across too keen in that situation. The art of seduction is an art for a reason. The cat-and-mouse, the thrill of the chase, and all that. She's into us, sure. Time to give her something back. I give her a wave back and, yep, you guessed it, she walks over.

SARAH WOOD: *My mate Adam was stood behind him. I was teaching at the time. I'd just finished university in Manchester and was working at a local school with Adam. So, I wave at Adam and suddenly I've got two lads waving back at us.*

Of course, I say I gave her a wave back – I was frantically waving, like I was hailing down a cab at 2 a.m. in the rain. I turn around and there's only another bloke there waving back at her. I turn back, she's already passed me and hugging him. I felt like an absolutely numpty. Here I was, trying to play it cool, and I was as cringe as anything.

Later on in the night, she went to the bar by herself so if we did start talking, I knew it was to us. So I got up and went to the bar. I sidle up to her and try to retain my cool demeanour with the line: 'You were pulling some moves over there, weren't ya?' Not great, but it did the trick. She asked why I wasn't out there and I said I was more of a chill-at-the-bar kinda guy. 'You know, I'm kind of a big deal,' I say, leaning up against the bar, swirling my cordial.

SARAH WOOD: *It probably sounds daft, but I was impressed he wasn't drinking alcohol. I was thinking, he hasn't got any drink in him to come over with a bit of courage to start chatting us up. Totally sober, off his own back. I actually found that quite attractive. It probably made us like him more. That night I took that away as a positive.*

I didn't know this at the time, but other people had been trying to set us up that night. A family friend of hers came over and asked if she had her eye on anyone, and Sarah's mam apparently pointed to me and said, 'Oh, she likes him!' So this family friend decided then and there to set us up. At the time, I was thinking, 'Why is Janet coming over asking if I'm single?' Now I know.

Our first date was a couple of months later. I had just gotten off an A tour and she was a schoolteacher. I had some time off so played it cool for a couple of days. You know, texty-texty, flirty-flirty, texty-texty. Build it up. I'm not a caveman. You know, try to play it cool but really you're as keen as mustard.

I saw her the next weekend for this date at an Italian and then into Toon (Newcastle) to this bar with live music. This time I decided to take the initiative and pulled her up to dance. She went, 'Ah, nae one ever does that.' And I looked at her and said, 'Well, when you've got the rhythm, you just cannit help it. When tha shoulders start going and the hips kick in, it's allowa red rover.'

It wasn't all smooth going, though. The first time I went to get up to use the bathroom in the restaurant, I walked into a mirror.

GLEN TAYLOR: *Not to stitch him up or anything, but Woody was good at everything except with girls. He might be the only seventeen-year-old who has ever sent an email to a girl saying, 'hi how r u?' Granted, Jonny Storey and I egged him on to do it, like we did with that Armani shirt. But come on, man. It's not old school or new school – it was just ridiculous. I think he got her email off MSN Messenger.*

MARK WOOD: *How good was MSN Messenger, by the way? It was like what WhatsApps are now. There was one stage where me and Woakesy were only communicating through MSN Messenger abbreviations: BRB (be right back), ASL (age, sex, location), things like that.*

CHRIS WOAKES: *We were also talking about how we both used to give it the big one on MSN at night: speaking to girls from school, chirping away and then literally not* *even looking at them at school the next day because we were too scared.*

WOOD: *Remember there was that option where it would show you what song you were listening to? Mine had the same song over and over because it was the only song I had on my iTunes. It was 50 Cent and The Game. I couldn't be further away from Compton.*

It's the blessing and curse of living in a small town. Everyone knew everyone else's business, and that's still the case. At the same time, you have situations like this, where people are looking out for you, trying to match-make. I definitely got lucky with Sarah, even though we lived around the corner and her garden pretty much opened up onto the cricket club.

With Sarah, it was perfect from the start. Even how we met that night, it seemed to be the perfect moment. The fact that we were from the same area and our families knew each other. It was destined to be. We had a lot of friends in common, even some of our family knew each other well. I said in my wedding speech: 'Me auntie Carol was in your uncle Andy's class at school, even though me auntie looks younger (got to have her back, don't I?). Your dad and my dad went to the same school in the same year. We lived around the corner, we're both from Ashington. Well, Sarah, if we're related it's too late now. But we'll probably have kids that can breathe under water.'

With Sarah it was meant to be. We fell in love pretty quickly, had Harry and built a loving family. With them, my family and my mates, I feel like my life is full of a lot of love.

★

Do I love cricket? It's a tricky question to answer, certainly when I think back to what cricket meant to me when I was younger. I loved playing it, I loved playing at Ashington. The thing about those two things was that what I loved about both was my friends.

I loved being out all day and playing with my mates, and I suppose cricket was the best vehicle for doing that. You're out in the sun, having fun, trying to do your best for each other.

The more I think back to those moments, the more I realize what were the real driving forces. I wasn't thinking about how much I wanted to be a professional or represent my country, I was just thinking about hanging out with people I liked. Even when we were just driving around town people-watching, or having sleepovers where, admittedly, I was going to be asleep at 9.30 p.m. when everyone was staying up until way past midnight, you were just doing things to be around others.

Cricket was basically my happy place. I had a sense of belonging. That changed a bit when I started going up the levels. It definitely got more exciting. I still remember when I first got in the Durham team in 2011, I was thinking, 'This is it!' Looking back, I was probably nowhere near a good enough skill level to be there. I trained well, sure, but I wasn't as dedicated. I just played to play, and representing Durham was an extension of playing for Ashington because you were playing for your region, and Durham is the kind of region where there is a real togetherness.

We're that little bit further away in the North East from other counties. Durham were the newest first-class county for seventy years when we first played in the County Championship in 1992. Since then, we've won it three times, and I was chuffed to play a few games the last time we did, in 2013. We've won a few limited-overs trophies, too.

When I first came into the group, I couldn't believe some of the people we were around. I was sharing a dressing room with proper players, like Paul Collingwood, Dale Benkenstein, Phil Mustard and Graham Onions. At the time, I was playing a lot of second-team cricket with the likes of Callum Thorp, Mitch Claydon and Neil Killeen. Neil was a huge help to us when he moved into coaching. Sometimes you can come into a place like that as a new kid and feel like the older guys are against you, because you're pretty much there to eventually take their spots. But they couldn't have been more welcoming in their own ways. Onions used to give me his bowling boots, talk through bowling with us, help me with my skills and what he felt it took to be a dedicated professional, which was huge considering he was such a good bowler for England. I still remember him bowling out Mike Hussey in 2009. It was also great that Harmy was still around when I got started and would give me lifts and make sure I felt at home as a fellow Ashington lad. So did his brother, Ben, who I always looked up to as the superstar. He had so much talent, probably more than Steven.

We ended up growing a pretty special Durham side, with established talent and youngsters like myself coming through, many of us from the local area. I still remember this game we played in 2013 against Yorkshire in the County Championship. We beat them by seven wickets, which essentially got us the title off the back of it. Paul Collingwood, who was our captain, said the game was more like a Test match than some of the 68 Test matches he played in. The standard was so high and you could see that from the players who took part: Colly, Ben Stokes, Phil Mustard, Mark Stoneman, Keaton Jennings and myself had either played international cricket at the time or would go on to do so. The Yorkshire side was similar: Adam Lyth, Phil Jaques (eleven Test caps for Australia), Kane Williamson (currently one of the best batters in the world for New Zealand), Jonny Bairstow, Gary Ballance, Adil Rashid, Liam Plunkett and Ryan Sidebottom.

A lot of the younger players in our group had learned

from the big names at Durham when we were coming through. One of those was Michael Di Venuto, the Australian batter who was a proper legend up here. He was the man at Durham and I still call him The King whenever I see him. When he retired he said to me, 'You can have my seat and my locker,' which was a huge honour. I know it's just somewhere to sit and a few pegs, but dressing-room space is a big deal. It was as if he'd handed me his sword to look after when he passed into the new realm or something.

Then there were people like Ottis Gibson, Gareth Breese (a Welshman who played international cricket for West Indies) and players like West Indies legend Shivnarine Chanderpaul as our overseas players.

Shiv was one of a kind, a left-handed batter who played for his country across twenty-one years. He had one of the most unusual batting stances around, standing chest-on to you when, traditionally, people stand side-on. He'd also have this trigger movement where he'd walk across his stumps, which made him even more unusual. I used to bowl at him in the nets and often he'd stop us and give advice. A regular one was that I kept trying to get the ball to go across him, which is a pretty common thing for right-arm bowlers like myself to do. He'd be like, 'No, don't do that – you're bowling lovely shape getting the ball in to me. Keep bowling with that shape, man.' Yeah right, I will, if you say so!

It was great watching Chanderpaul train. The first team would train before us and then we'd come in as the second XI and bowl at them after. There was one day he was on the bowling machine and he only had his front pad on. It was set to like 90-odd mph and he was crunching them down the ground every ball. I remember thinking, if this is what it takes to make that standard, I'm never going to make it.

I was just surrounded by these giants of the game, and I looked up to them so much that every day I'd think about pulling out my autograph book before my kit. And that was kind of the problem.

I remember the moment it all switched. John Windows, one of my main academy coaches, came up to us one day and said I need to think of this more like a job. Every time you put your pads on or strap on your bowling boots, you're putting on a suit and tie to go into work. You have to treat it that seriously. At the time I still had vibes that it was a hobby. This was fun, not serious. So many people would give up everything to be a professional cricketer. And I knew that, but my main focus was enjoying it because, heck, I was one of the lucky ones.

John was tough on us at times. Sometimes when I'm struggling on the field, I'll hear his voice in the back of my head going. 'Ah, Woody, why can't you just hit the top of off stump?!' He used to go hard at us in the nets when I was batting, throwing hundreds and hundreds of short balls at us because he knew I hated it. There were a few times when I'd throw my bat and gloves down, along with a few toys out of the pram, and shout back, 'Why are you doing this?!' Then you're playing against Australia or India, and Mitchell Starc or Jasprit Bumrah are flinging balls down at your neck and you realize, ah yeah, fair play, John. You were just preparing me for the real world. Likewise, Geoff Cook and Alan Walker were excellent with us when I got into the first team. Hard but fair. Any praise would be a drop in the ocean compared to the work they drilled into us. It was all meant well; it just didn't seem that way at the time.

There was a lot of tough love at Durham. One time John had us diving on mud heaps off the side of the ground in the pouring rain to work on our fielding. To finish the session, he took us out to the middle to do high catches, just as the wind had picked up and the rain was coming down harder. The rule was you weren't allowed inside, where there was hot soup waiting, until you took one.

I managed to get a quick exit, but one of my teammates, a South African lad called Adam Shir, got the rough end. He wore glasses, you see, which meant every time the ball went in the air, he looked up and saw nothing through his drenched, streaky lenses. An hour passed by and we were all finishing our soup or getting seconds when someone said, 'Anyone seen Adam?' Not long after, he walked in, head, shoulders and arms battered and bruised. His hands were black and blue. But he took his catch eventually, and that's what mattered. That was the Durham way – being tough and not giving in.

Some people were still able to find ways around it. We used to do this 'river run' in preseason, which started with a lap of the ground at Chester-le-Street, out and along the banks of the river, then through the car park and back to the ground. Ben Raine, our allrounder, the genius that he is, decided to skip the running bit after coming out of the ground and went straight to an ice cream van. He bought an ice cream, enjoyed it at his leisure, then got a bottle of water to pour over his hair and face. After enough people had gone by, he rejoined for the last bit. He must have run 200 yards out of the five miles. And he got away with it. That's what you call working smart.

Of course, I do love the game now, and I love bowling fast. But it's a different kind of love: it comes through the honour of being able to do what so many people dream of doing. I've never lost the fun of it. It's just a bit more measured now, a bit more grown up. When I first started playing for Durham and England, if I had a bad day I'd be on the floor, and on a good day I was flying up the walls.

Obviously, there are bad days when you bowl crap and that. I still have that. But it's still great fun. Playing at Lord's – how good's that? Cape Town? Sydney? Ha-way man, it's unreal. But playing for Ashington will always be my first love. It was when I was my most contented.

When I first signed for Durham I became a 'pro'. It meant I couldn't play for Ashington any more because the club would sign a pro who was available for the whole season, while I could only play eight or nine games because of the commitments of my contract. The rules stated you were only allowed to have one pro per club, and Ashington needed someone available for the whole season. I had to go and play for South Northumberland, Tynemouth and Tynedale. It wasn't the same and it really made me realize what Ashington meant to me, that it was more than just a place I played cricket.

If England would let me, I'd play for Ashington tomorrow.

JONNY STOREY: *Before the World Cup semi-final against Australia, there were club nets on and we looked over and this bloke was bowling out in the middle, watched by his dad. Some people were like, 'Hold on – is that Woody? Is he not playing in a World Cup?' Even when I drive home with my wife after we've been out, we'll drive past People's Park and my wife will go, 'Hang on, is that Woody?' Yep, it's him, doing shuttle runs on a bit of green at the top of his parents' road while his dad's holding a stopwatch. He's got access to the fanciest gyms and facilities in the world, and he's still doing all his elite training in Ashington!*

MARK WOOD: *Aye, I've got everything I could ever need here.*

When Sarah and I started dating, she'd often come and watch me play. It was a pretty great feeling, to be honest. We get a lot of excellent support in England and abroad, and everyone's always willing us on to do well, singing your name and applauding you when you walk back down to fine leg after bowling a good over or spell. But it's a pretty cool feeling when you know there are some people there just for you. I love seeing my family and mates in the crowd, especially when it takes a bit of time to pick them out. That moment you see their faces and they're cheering or even just waving back lifts you. Harry's too young at the moment to fully get what I do, but I have these videos Sarah does of him shouting 'Come on, Daddy!' when I come up on TV.

She was around cricket a lot but she wasn't really that into it. I don't know if that helped when we first started dating, but I'm not sure it would have mattered either way. I'm sure she was with me for my good looks and great chat.

Now she properly gets into it. When I saw her right after we'd won the World Cup final, she was white as a sheet. Apparently, she'd been shouting all the way through, standing on chairs, almost falling off the balcony of the England box she was in because she was getting into it that much. A few of the other families had to try and get her to sit down. Which makes sense because she was six months pregnant at the time. Apparently when I came out to bat with Stokesy, she was screaming, '*Run! Just run! Do you even need your bat – just fling it past the line!*' To be honest, I'm sure the rest of the country were thinking the same.

SARAH WOOD: *The first year I started seeing Mark was the first time he got picked for England, in 2015. Going to see him play in the Ashes that summer was my first experience of the Ashes, or any cricket for England. I was still picking up the rules, working out who the players were. When he got his first wicket of that Ashes series, I jumped up and shouted, 'Yes! Get in!' from the balcony. Two of the girls I was with in the box were telling us to be quiet. 'You don't go on like that. It's not a football match.' I got told off for cheering him! I'm a bit more calm now. I always keep an eye out for the speedometer to see how fast his balls are, and how many records he's going to try and break.*

As annoying as my injuries have been, they did help us at the start because it meant a few winters at home so we could spend more time together. But once I started playing regularly, things got harder.

That's probably one of the toughest things about playing cricket for England. You're always leaving people at home. It's been great when Sarah comes out with Harry, but that just means you feel it that little bit more when they're not there. You end up being in a long-distance relationship half the year, as well as being an absentee father.

SARAH: *The long periods, and not being able to travel during Covid, I found that quite hard. That long-distance relationship is really hard, especially with a little one. I hate saying it but I feel a little bit like a single parent because I'm making all these decisions by myself without the support of Mark. For those lengths of time, I get to a point where I'm desperate for him to get back.*

She says that, but the first week back is always tricky. Sarah gets in a routine with Harry, and I usually come in and mess it up. I would say you can match up the biggest disagreements we've had with that first week back. It takes some adjusting, but we work it out.

When I'm away, I always make sure to speak to Sarah twice a day, once in the morning and once in the evening. It's never chats about anything really beyond our days. We never argue over the phone, because really there's nothing ever to argue about. Also, there's no point doing that over the phone.

Talking things through always helps, and I say that as someone who probably hasn't done that enough in the past. Professionally, too, communication is so important, particularly off the field. I hate being dropped and hate being rested for England, but I always respect when either Morgy or Rooty, even Cookie earlier, would take the time to explain their decisions to us. I'd still be annoyed, but at least I had clarity.

The same goes for on the field, too. There needs to be a bit of back-and-forth, and probably early on in my career I was so keen to make a good impression that I went along with plans when I could have been used better. Now that I've got a bit of confidence and earned more trust, I feel like I can put my side across on the field and in meetings. In an ODI against India at Headingley in July 2018, Rashid got Suresh Raina out caught leg slip. The ball before, I had said to Jos that the way Raina – a left-hander – was trying to work the ball around the corner against the spin, do you not think we should have someone in close there? Next ball he turned it into the hands of leg slip. Jos and Morgy had a little celebration together and I remember thinking, 'You're joking, Jos – I was the one who told you that!'

My relationship with Root went through the roof when he became Test captain. We always got on but, even though he's one of the best batters in the world, my respect for him went up with the way he carried himself with the England captaincy. I really felt for him when the results weren't going his way, even though he was scoring century after century. You see the way he carried all that responsibility, especially during Covid, and still performed – it felt gutting that we could not hit the same standards.

The day before he stepped down as captain, he called me to let me know. It was bittersweet. I was sad that he felt he had to step away from something he loved doing. At the same time, I was glad he felt comfortable with the situation. He talked about how captaincy had started to filter into other parts of his life and was making him miserable. He sounded at peace with his decision, and I admired him even more for that. I feel lucky to have played under him and am looking forward to him breaking a few more records now he can just bat. He's the kind of player I'm going to tell Harry all about when he's older. I love him as a bloke, which is something my mates often ridicule me for because I'd do anything for him.

SEAN 'SHEEP' MCCAFFERTY: *We always joke that Woody used to run errands for Rooty just to get an England cap. We were in Manchester the night before the India Test in 2021 that got postponed, eating in Wagamama. At the end of the meal, Woody got a text from Root, asking if he could bring some food back for him. Unfortunately, Woody had to order it in front of us and we had to hammer him for that. 'Is the only reason you're playing tomorrow because you're the captain's personal Deliveroo driver?' To be fair, I'd walk a chicken katsu curry down from Ashington for an England cap, so fair play.*

MARK WOOD: *Well, Rooty and I have a good relationship with food. In St Lucia in 2019, he'd invited us to his*

I got the new Wimbledon kit off Santa. Straight to the garden.

Me mam used to hate getting her picture taken – me, not so much.

Batting at the Kenilworth Road Oval (aka the back garden).

I know what you're thinking, but it's not Ant & Dec. It's the oldest looking 11-year-old (Jonny Storey) with the youngest looking 11-year-old (me).

At national finals with Ashington Under13s, at the poshest school ever (Oakham), with Sean McCafferty aka Sheep (right) and Chris Watson (left).

Taking the wicket to win the Ashes in 2015.

'Alright Finny, I get it.'

Letting it fly in St Lucia. One of my quickest spells this, I reckon.

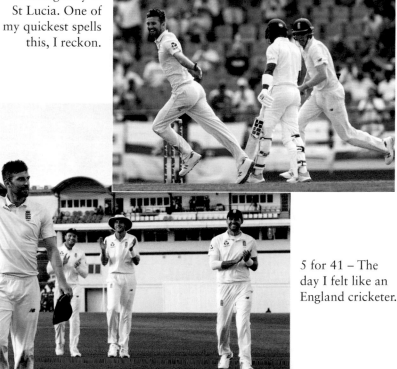

5 for 41 – The day I felt like an England cricketer.

Touring South Africa and knocking stumps out of the ground – two of my favourite things.

One of me favourites: backroom staff, players and ex-players all celebrating in the dressing room after our 2020 series win in South Africa.

Winning away in Australia – doesn't get any better than that.

The need for speed.

'Hard lines mate. If only you could have hit it wide of long on.'

Series win in Sri Lanka with Jos Buttler and a trophy shaped like a moose.

Introducing the lads to the team song that me and Jos wrote on his bat after winning the 2019 World Cup at Lord's (PS: check whose spot that is in the corner).

The set-up for proposing to Sarah.

I held up my part of the deal, Ed. I want my guitar!

Live show with Middle Please, Umpire at Miles Jupp's cricket club, Monmouth.

Acupuncture with Ben Langley. He later told me he'd never trained in acupuncture before…

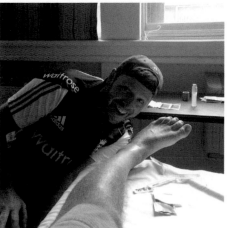

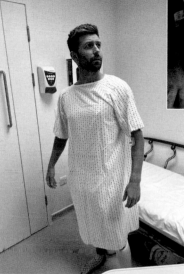

Pre-surgery before the anaesthetic shenanigans kick in.

Bio-bubble dinner date with Chris Woakes and some dodgy haircuts (PS: how much does Wiz look like Captain America?).

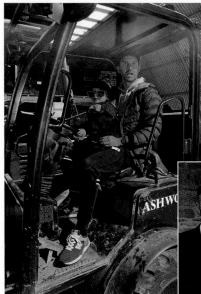

Absolutely digger mad with my son, Harry.

Smart as a dart with the family: Mam, Dad and wor Sarah.

2015, celebrating the Ashes win in the Oval dressing room with me best mates Glen Taylor, Scott Dunn, Jonny Storey and Josh Robinson.

room to tell us I was playing and talk me through what he expected and how I was feeling about playing because it was a bit of a last-chance-saloon type thing as I'd changed my run-up and needed to make the opportunity count. We ended up watching a movie together and having a burger. I got those nine wickets in that game.

JOE ROOT: *Yeah, you bowled like the speed of light! You can be quite a nervous character sometimes, especially preparing for games so it was just a case of trying to keep you as relaxed as possible. Because you worry about absolutely everything - things you shouldn't worry about at all.*

WOOD: *Every night I was back in your room having food and playing Mario Kart because I was superstitious.*

ROOT: *Yeah it was funny movies, then Mario Kart. Though Mario Kart ended up getting quite serious so maybe it wasn't a great idea during Test matches.*

WOOD: *I'd knock on the door and be like, 'Rooty, can I come in?' And he'd be, 'Oh for f... Yeah, fine.' I liked that dynamic because going out is fun but so is just chilling out in someone's room.*

ROOT: *Even if we'd had a rough day, you'd either come around to mine or I'd go around to yours. We'd generally try and have each other's back, so it was a nice way of furthering our friendship. We've managed to keep each other sane. Well as sane as it's possible to keep you, anyway.*

WOOD: *Did you not mind me coming over as often as I did?*

ROOT: *It was a two-way thing because it definitely helped me, too. Captaincy can be a very lonely place sometimes and it was always nice having someone around. You do get that feeling on occasion where you end up finding people that you've always been quite close with distancing themselves slightly from you because of your position in the team as a captain. It never felt that way at all with you. You really helped me out when I needed you to, without having to ask.*

WOOD: *I didn't see you as anything other than someone I was friends with. Before you were captain, you were me mate. And I don't think any other past England captains would have let me have as much pudding before a Test.*

As for Morgy, I think I can attribute all my success in white ball cricket to him. The trust, respect, the loyalty and success I've got – that's all on Morgy. He saw value in us. I've got so much admiration for how he is as a person. He has a bigger perspective on life, and that's helped a few of us be not so up and down with cricket, and also helped him be one of the lads while being our talismanic captain.

He never, ever stutters when he speaks. There are no 'ermm', 'obviously', 'you know' – all the words you might use to join up sentences while you're thinking about what you're saying. It's so clear, so thorough and to the point. He says it because he means it and it's so clear and to the point.

The amount of times I've heard him say: 'All right lads, that's a par score – one partnership should win us this game'. No matter how I've bowled, whether they've got 350, 300 or 250, it was par. With that, he'd just take all the pressure off you. Though my favourite Morgy quote is 'Get in, ya little dixie!' which he always says whenever you get a wicket.

He's only got angry with us twice. Once, as I mentioned, when I volleyed the ball past the stumps in the T20 World Cup. The other time was when I pulled Dawid Malan's pants down in a New Zealand airport when he had nae undercrackers on. Both times he just said, 'That's not good, boss', which is enough of a telling off from Morgy.

I suppose whether it's captains, coaches or your partner, all relationships take work. They don't just go along at the same level where everything's perfect. Even your mates who you've known for your whole life, you can't take them for granted by getting lost in your own world because you think it's more important.

We all spend a lot less time with each other because life moves on and we've all got our own lives and stuff to be dealing with. That's why one of my favourite things is getting messages from my mates when I'm playing. They'll always message before and after a day's play, often with feedback and honesty, especially if I've bowled rubbish. But they're always checking in and I always try to do the same.

SEAN 'SHEEP' MCCAFFERTY: *It is easy to send a message to say well done, but I like to think we're more conscious of messaging him when it isn't going well. Sometimes not to say anything about cricket, just to ask him how he is.*

JONNY STOREY: *For the last Test tour to South Africa, Sarah wasn't going out, and I was around at Woody's a few days before and he was pretty down. All of a sudden he goes, 'Well, why don't you come?' I looked at him, looked at Sarah, who shrugged saying I might as well, and then at my wife who, let's just say, wasn't best pleased. That night, Woody sent me his itinerary and highlighted a week where I should come to Cape Town. I ended up going with my dad, who might be Woody's biggest fan. He didn't play that match, but his face when we got to his hotel on that first day was priceless. Being able to give him that lift meant a lot. My wife still hasn't forgiven me, mind.*

THE FAMILY WHISTLE

Some people have family tartan. Some people have a family song. I have a family whistle. Not like a fancy silver one, like a referee, but a tune with your lips. *Peep-peeeep*, as hard as that is to imagine in print.

The key to a family whistle is it has to be short but recognizable. It has to cut through the general hum of wherever you are. When you hear it, it should give you a feeling of comfort and put you at ease. Your tribe are near by and you are safe.

It's not for fighting purposes, like. This isn't like some war cry or a bugle. After all, hearing a whistle like ours is hardly going to get your enemies fleeing. It's just a way of knowing your people are among you.

GLEN TAYLOR: *You can do it anywhere and his head starts wobbling, looking for where it's coming from. We've been at cricket grounds and done it from the stands and he's on the field, looking around. He'll be playing in the Ashes, and he'll do it back and we'll reply so he can work out where we are. Even in a massive series where he's got to be dead serious, he'll do it just to acknowledge his mates.*

It can also work as an alarm clock.

DANIEL GRANT: *We would go for cricket training every Saturday morning and he'd come out of his house and do the whistle he does all the time just before we needed to walk down to the club, which was about a minute away. I could hear him through my bedroom window, which was 200 yards away. I'd be half asleep and hear him and think, ah Christ, gear on and stumble out of my house and get there before him.*

Of course, you need to be consistent with it, because it won't stick straight away. That way you can pass it on for generations, as it has been to me.

SARAH: *It's from Mark's side of the family, so I feel honoured to be part of it now. Mark will do it to me when we're out shopping so I know where he is. It's much easier than getting on the tannoy and telling them I've lost my husband. Harry's attuned to it now – his ears perk up whenever he hears it.*

The danger is always that someone outside the tribe might use it against you. I have a habit of doing it when I'm not really thinking. I'll be in the changing room or out in the middle when we're fielding and you're in your own head. It's slipped out a few times and someone picked up on it. One time I did it in the changing rooms in Australia, which is relevant because their changing rooms are huge. All of a sudden, someone did it back and I was looking around but couldn't pin it on anyone. It happened a few more times so I decided to do it and look around immediately to see who replied. It turns out it was Jos. He was the first to crack the code.

JOS BUTTLER: *I think it's his and Sarah's way of flirting with each other. It comes in handy though when you catch him drifting. He'll start veering away from where he's supposed to be fielding and you can whistle at him and he'll pick up on it and start paying attention again.*

Ultimately, it's just a little something that reinforces your bond with those close to you. A couple of peeps that either lets people know you're around for them, or they're around for you. A little expression of your love for those who hear it. Even Jos.

★

I knew I was going to marry Sarah very soon after we moved in together. I'd never lived with anyone before at that point. In fact, I used to get fined regularly at the club for being the richest man in Ashington still living with his mam and dad. There was probably a time when I was the only international cricketer whose mam packed his bag. When I started living with Sarah, she tried her best to help me like Mam did but it didn't work out. She was folding my tops all funny and didn't have things in the right order. She gave me an ultimatum that I had to accept how she did things, and that it would be different to Mam. I've been packing them myself since then.

My main problem was I couldn't cook. Mam used to do it all and, to be honest, it took a lot to leave that behind. I tried my hardest at first. I even bought the Joe Wicks cookbook. I think the first proper meal I did for us – romantic, like – was steak and chips. For some reason, I wanted to make the chips from scratch. I mean, it looks pretty easy: chop potatoes, cook them – chips! But I'd never peeled one before. My only previous experience with them were jacket potatoes, which was every second meal at the start of us living together. I had to FaceTime Storey to talk me through it. The onions were a debacle, too. Again, I'd never done it before and found out people weren't joking about the tears. I had to wear goggles.

Cooking, though, was my way of giving a bit more to Sarah. I wanted to get it right to try and pay her back for all she does for us. Not just with Harry, but supporting me as well. Even though there was a lot of trial and error at first, and for her a lot of swallowing without chewing at the start, I feel like I've got better at it. I'm not saying I'm Gordon Ramsay over here, but I'm more comfortable in the kitchen than I used to be.

Saying that, though, in 2019 I won the best chef award at Chance To Shine's 'Chance to Dine' night at Lord's. There were four of us on the night and we had to make a nice meal for 180 guests dining in the Long Room, and at the end a panel of experts judged the dishes. Captain Morgy was up first with the canapés of lemon sole goujons, smoked mackerel pâté and tomato bruschetta. Tom Curran was on mains, roast sirloin beef accompanied by garlic cream-braised potatoes, green beans, carrots and a port jus. Pudsy (Liam Plunkett) closed it out at the death with mandarin parfait served with a blood-orange sorbet. Unfortunately, none of them could come close to my ham hock terrine with haggis, piccalilli and quail's egg. I'd love to give you a recipe but, you know what they say, chefs never reveal their secrets. Or is that magicians?

But yeah, I knew Sarah was the one for me pretty early on. I think when you know you can live with someone, you know you can spend the rest of your life with them. I know I'm not the easiest person to live with, so the fact she wanted to meant a lot. She still hates it when I sing. Or specifically, 'over sing'. She always asks why I can't sing nicely, why I always go over the top. But that's because whenever I sing, I imagine myself in a music video and have to give it my all, like I'm auditioning for *The Greatest Showman*. I used to think she was the one with the problem until Harry's started going 'Daddy, no singing. Stop.' Tough crowd.

SARAH: *I think that's the thing with Mark. He knows how to wind us up. But even that comes from a strength of knowing how to make people feel better.*

I had a very traumatic labour and ended up having an emergency C-section. Afterwards, me and Harry were both on antibiotics on a drip because during surgery we both got an infection. One night he couldn't stay so he had to go back home and return the next morning.

I don't know how, but he just knew exactly what I needed. The next day he arrived at 9 a.m. having been to Marks & Spencers to get loads of night gowns to wear in hospital because I didn't have any. I only had pyjamas but I couldn't wear the bottoms after having surgery. They had buttons as well for breast-feeding. I don't know why that even occurred to him to get them. I didn't know he'd be so attentive to those little things. He also got a sandwich from my favourite place because he'd known I was in labour for twenty-six hours and hadn't eaten much. I remember thinking, 'Thank you, so much.' The thought he put in to getting all these things. And the sandwich made my day.

★

Now, I know people get bored of hearing other people's proposal stories, but if you're reading standing up, you're going to want to sit down for this.

It was 1 August 2017, the day before Sarah's birthday. I'd saved up for a ring but decided I needed a big statement before asking her to marry us. I got her to leave the house in the morning to go shopping, which was a bit tricky because she had tonsillitis. I practically had to kick her out the door and I got the feeling she was very hacked off with us, which was not a great start.

I'd decided to set up the hallway to our house with candles on tables leading to the doors to our living room. There were six tables in total, and on each table were drawings of different scenes from our favourite times together done by a mate of mine who is an artist: of the first time we met at the cricket club, when we cycled around Hyde Park, from a trip to New York, our first James Bay concert, of us sat on Hadrian's Wall and, lastly, of me proposing to her.

As soon as she came home, I played a cover of 'Can't Help Falling In Love' by Haley Reinhart. I could tell she was surprised: the 'Mark... what's gan on?' was a giveaway. She took her time getting through the hallway, which felt like an age given I was on one knee at this point. Then she got to that last picture and gasped. She opened the door slowly and saw me knelt down with a smug look on my face. Will you marry us?

To some of you, that might sound a bit familiar. Because, well, I took that whole idea from a Wrigley's Extra Gum advert. Even the music. The advert is basically this guy and girl who had been together for a long time, had known each other since they were kids. They'd gan through life together and every time they had a significant moment together, they'd share a chewing gum and he'd drawn the event on the wrapper. She moves away, they have their highs and lows, and they eventually come back to meet each other and live happily ever after.

It's feels a bit cheesy to say, but I think that's most people's experience of love, and it was certainly ours. There are special moments and also times when you feel like you're being pulled apart, even when neither of you wants that. You always push through the tough times because of the better times ahead. Sometimes you do so because you hope there are, but with Sarah, it's because I know there are. And anyway, it's a bloody good advert. I've probably watched it on YouTube more times than us winning the World Cup.

5

HOW TO TRAVEL

One of the main reasons cricket is brilliant is that it's a summer sport. As an international cricketer, you are chasing the sun to all corners of the world and being paid well to do it. We get flown out to some of the most exotic places in the world in business class, get put up in stunning hotels and are always treated amazingly wherever we go. Everyone gives us a brilliant welcome (even in Australia) and the locals are always accommodating (yes, even in Australia).

Yes, the schedule is packed, and there are years where I've spent more time abroad than at home with my family, even during the pandemic when travel was restricted for so many people across the world. But we get all the frills, visit some of the best destinations in the world, all to play cricket for our country. Aside from being the head taste tester for Ferrero Rocher, I reckon I've got one of the best jobs in the world.

There is one, small, teensy-tiny problem: I'm not a good flyer. The idea of it still blows my mind. Just going up in the air to thirty thousand feet for hours on end, over land and sea. I mean, I get how 'travel' works. But planes? I've been on hundreds of them by now but I'm still nowhere near being completely zen on them.

I'm just about OK on the big planes now because you don't feel the bumps, plus you've got room in business class so you don't feel so claustrophobic in this metal tube shooting through the sky. But I can never really decide on the best way to make myself feel at ease. I don't just want to stay in my seat because I'll think about being trapped in the air and get anxious. At the same time, if I get up I'll end up pacing up and down, bumping into stewards and taking out the drinks carts. They'll probably end up restraining me after that and that'll be even worse.

Hands down the worst flight I've ever been on was with Jimmy Anderson when he and I were flying out to a training camp in La Manga, Spain. To get there, we arrived into Alicante, where there is no space between where the sea ends and the tarmac begins. We were about to make our initial landing when the plane pulled up at the last second. I grabbed Jimmy so hard I thought I'd broken his hand. Imagine that in the papers the next week: 'ENGLAND LEGEND OUT WITH BROKEN HAND AFTER WET WIPE WOOD LANDING SHAME'.

Apparently it's quite a common thing, but I thought there was something wrong with the plane. The wheels had broken or something and we couldn't land. What are we going to do? We're going to have to land in the sea? What if a shark comes and attacks us? I'm going to have to fight him off here. I was thinking of all these things that could go wrong. Not even a neck pillow could sort us out at that point. We landed the second time and I vowed to never get on a plane again. I was preparing for my new life in Spain.

Places like the Caribbean and New Zealand are pretty nerve-racking because you have to get on these small little propeller planes to hop from one island to the other. Sure, people talk about the beautiful beaches. But no one mentions the propeller planes! That's probably when my flying fear is at its worst. I need to be sat with people who understand us: lead physio Ben Langley, team masseur/ manager Mark Saxby, our strength and conditioning coach Phil Scott, the team doctor or sympathetic teammates like David Willey, Chris Woakes or Keaton Jennings. They can distract me, talk me through it.

Then there are the people who deliberately go out of their way to wind us up. Ottis Gibson was a nightmare because he'd laugh it off as if I'm being soft. I'm clinging on to the seat and he's slapping my knee saying, 'Oooops, we're going to go down, Woody!' Stokesy will be the same. One time I was sat with him, panicking as we were rattling about in a bad bit of turbulence. I was all over the place while he was just enjoying it. 'If we die, we die,' he said, cackling. How is that helpful?

CHRIS WOAKES: *Because of how they do the arrangements on the plane in alphabetical order, we are always sat next to each other. To say you're an iffy flyer is putting it mildly. I've got to know your tics and how to get you calm.*

MARK WOOD: *I've got it down to a tee now. I listen to meditation when I first get on, to help with my anxiety. I have certain songs I listen to. I try to mix it up: some oldies, preferably rock. But if it's too upbeat that would send us out too. Nothing too mellow like Dido, but just pleasant stuff: Train, James Bay. Acoustic, less hyped-up. Just to chill out. Absolutely nothing to do with anything I'm trying to avoid: 'Fallin' by Alicia Keys, 'Crash' by Usher, none of that would be in there. I've got my drink, sweets or chewing gum, and migraine tablets. I have a game called Word Cookies on my phone that I'll do as we're taking off. Distractions, basically.*

WOAKES: *Yeah, I know about your music. There's also the ridiculous thing you do of wearing sunnies on a plane, which makes you look even more daft when you're pretending to play the drums to whatever you're listening to. I remember that fidget spinner as well. I can't imagine what other people getting on the plane are thinking when you're playing with this thing designed for ten-year-olds while I'm holding your hand.*

WOOD: *Those fidget spinners were great. The amount I span mine, it was like a third propeller. I actually got that from Pudsy because he read somewhere that it was good for distracting you. He's also a ridiculously nervous flyer. I* *still remember one time we got off a flight from Barbados to St Kitts on one of those tiny planes and he had sweated through his England suit.*

★

I was always pretty wary of being far from home. Even now, I have a set routine for getting back into home life. Sarah has it down to a tee.

SARAH WOOD: *Aye, I'll take this one. He'll walk in the door and spend every second of the day making it up to Harry: whether going swimming, taking him to the beach. He loves his blankets, so he gets them set up on the settee with whatever he wants to watch on the television. We have to have a full fridge and, of course, a box of Ferrero Rochers. He'll then go to his mam's and she'll make him broth, jacket potatoes, his mam's Sunday dinners. He craves Sunday dinners. He'd probably have that every day if he could.*

MARK WOOD: *Me mam's broth is the best thing since sliced bread. It's got white onions, barley, carrots, split pea, swede, stock and a thick gammon joint. Honestly, if someone said to me you could eat your mam's broth for starter, having a Sunday lunch for your main and choco-late fudge cake with custard for dessert, I wouldn't get sick of it.*

Ashington was where I wanted to be at all times, and that's still the case now. That's fairly normal, I reckon. When you grow up somewhere like here, your roots are so strong you don't feel like you need to be anywhere else. I knew the world was bigger beyond this small town, but I was never in a rush to see it. Playing for Northumberland, which wasn't too far away from home, and then moving on to Durham – moving beyond those surroundings happened in stages, which helped. Each felt like a bit-by-bit step.

I never really wanted to go out of my comfort zone. I never really wanted to gan to winter trials for North of England, part of the regional cricket pathway you go through at age-group level, because I didn't really know anyone. I never wanted to go to the England Under-19s, even though I felt I should have been picked for that team.

I did train with the Under-19s as a net bowler, and when I got there I thought I was as good as them and wanted to prove a point. I wasn't a name to look out for and I didn't have a squad number. It was an incredibly talented group: Stokesy, Bairstow, James Vince. Nathan Buck (now of Northamptonshire) and Hamza Riazuddin (who was on the books at Hampshire) were the opening bowlers. Rooty was there but didn't play, so he and I ended up doing twelfth-man duties. I felt I was good enough, quicker than those playing county cricket at a young age at the time. But I was never going to get a look-in because they didn't rate us. And at the same time, I didn't want to go there and embarrass myself.

We used to play quite a bit for Northumberland against other counties. Northumberland, while it's OK in size, doesn't have many people living in it. There was also a fair bit of politics that came with picking those representative teams. Ashington was the club team in Northumberland that would always win everything, but there'd only be two or three players from us, when you could easily have six or seven. You'd always have to have at least one or two from the posh clubs. As a result, we'd never really win. We'd get pumped whenever we played bigger counties with a larger catchment area, like Lancashire and Yorkshire. We had to basically bowl first each time to make a game of it.

Around that time, my only exposure to travel abroad was on holidays to Spain or Portugal. The furthest I'd been was a flight to Cyprus. I was this closeted northern lad. We'd often go on holiday with other families, which was always a laugh. Well, more often than not.

One time my family and Dunny's family were on holiday together in Mallorca. I must have been eight or nine, and going away with a mate was great fun. We'd do a bit of sailing, hang out at the beach. My favourite memory of that trip was being on a boat with Dad as the sun set. It was one of those moments you take in and feel completely contented. Unfortunately, not all of the trip was like that. Let's just say there was a bit of a diplomatic incident.

We were playing football on the beach one day when a German family came over and asked if they could join in. After a while, another English family came by and got involved, then another German family. Eventually, we had enough players for an eight-a-side England v Germany match.

Abilities and ages were mixed, but it was hotly contested. I felt like we controlled the game, knocking the ball about as well as you could on sand. There were moments of quality, some bad misses and, as always when you play football on a beach, a few misguided attempts at overhead kicks. All in all, it was played in good spirit. Until England held a 4-3 lead as the game was winding down.

Suddenly, Germany get a chance: this bloke breaks past our admittedly weary backline and squares it across goal to his son, who just has the goalkeeper – my dad – to beat. His shot is on target but with nowt behind it. Dad, being the selfless gent he is, realizes how big a moment this is for this kid. He deliberately puts in a dive the wrong way to let the ball in. The son peels away to celebrate, chased by his dad who catches up with him and lifts him up. The perfect end to a wonderful game. Dunny's dad, however, wasn't best pleased.

'What are you doing, Derek?! What was that?! Why have you let that in?!'

'Oh come on, John,' laughed my dad. 'He's four years old.'

'I know he's only four. But he's German!'

No word of a lie, Derek and John didn't say a word to each other for the rest of the holiday. I reckon John still hasn't forgiven him to this day.

★

I've come to learn the best thing about travel is meeting new people. There are some fantastic sights across the world that really take your breath away, scenes that make you stop and take it all in. Whether it's Table Mountain in Cape Town or Grenada, which is right up there for me. My parents came there for an ODI tour and we went around the spice market and the old fort with a tour guide called Randy. He would walk us around town and show me off to his mates – 'Look, it's England fast bowler Mark Wood!' I'd be high-fiving people and that, like I was some sort of trophy. It was class. As he kept telling us, everybody on the island knew Randy.

I love speaking to the locals, learning about customs in the area you're in and how people go about their lives. That personal connection gives you a much better feel for the place and paints a better picture of where you are and why things are the way they are. I feel like I can chat to anyone and, when they eventually get to grips with the accent, I'd like to think people enjoy chatting with me. On a pace programme to Sri Lanka, I got pally with their chief of police, who was organizing our security detail – a lovely man called Lalith. He still texts me now before matches to wish me luck. I'll always go out of my way and say thank you to people that help us when we're away, just to let them know we're grateful for what they do for us.

I've found people love to show you what their place is all about. As someone who always shouts about Ashington and the North East, it's nice when someone is as passionate about where they are from. Maybe not London, mind. People rave about London and, I'll be honest, it's not for me. Don't get me wrong, it's great for a week or so. I love going there for Test matches at Lord's and The Oval, two great venues (nowhere near as good as Chester-le-Street, mind) with very different atmospheres. There are really nice restaurants, you can enjoy the theatre and walk around and see the sights – all a nice change from home. But it's far too hectic and I find it quite unfriendly at times. I couldn't live there.

As for the London Underground, my god, I cannit go on it. I'd rather walk for three hours than spend twenty minutes on it. It's dirty, squashy, people don't speak to you. It's loud. I feel a bit motion sick on it. Sometimes players will take the Underground to head into a match, particularly at The Oval in south London. I'd rather sit in traffic for two hours. It's too dark and dingy. I suppose saying that shows I couldn't work down a mine.

It's not the most intimidating place I've been to, though it is up there. That award goes to Oakham School, this proper fancy boarding school in Leicestershire.

I was there for a national Under-13 tournament. Our Ashington side, which was basically all of my mates, had won the right to represent Northumberland and were excited to do so. We had a strong team and had performed really well against more established clubs in our region. Clubs with centres of excellence, state-of-the-art facilities, paid coaches – all turned over by some likely lads. It was an exciting period for us and we couldn't wait to do ourselves justice. Then we arrived at this place and were a bit overawed.

Immediately we felt like we didn't belong there. It wasn't a nice feeling. We were walking around the grounds of this place so confused. Do people really go to school here? Is this what schools are like down south? It was like we'd been transported to Hogwarts. The poshest place you've ever seen. We all had our own rooms, there was a big dining area where we had our meals. All the lawns were pristine – the kind you're not allowed to play sports on. Display lawns.

All the other teams had fancy kit and training tops, while we had these raggedy polo shirts, trying to fit in and look all smart and that. I know me and a few of the lads worried that we were out of our depth. The environment was overwhelming and we felt so out of place.

Collectively, though, we all just thought, sod this, just enjoy it. If we beat people, we beat people. Let's just have a good time while we were here. As you can imagine, that good time came at other people's expense.

If we weren't stealing yoghurts from breakfast and lobbing them around, we were playing cricket in the hallways until the sun came up. Where were our chaperones? I hear you wondering. Well, we had two: Stevie Williams and another coach, Matty Hetherington. They weren't exactly disciplinarians.

Stevie was probably the more responsible one, but at the time he had a bad back. Each night we had to help him into bed. That meant once we'd put him down on his mattress, which was on the floor, he needed our help to get back up. We'd tuck him in and then run amok. We'd play corridor cricket and use his door for the stumps, knowing he couldn't really do anything about it. We'd be there well into the small hours, shouting and appealing, every now and again hearing a muffled *'Pack it in and go to bed – it's 2 a.m. for Pete's sake!'*

Luckily we held our own on the field, against some proper cricketers from around the country, so Stevie didn't hold it against us. He did get a bit hacked off when one of us decided to see if the fire alarm would go off if he sprayed deodorant up at it. Of course, it did: the whole building was evacuated, every team out on the pavement outside. Fire engines turn up and he decides to come clean: 'Sorry, I was just spraying deodorant on my armpits.' I mean, you'd have to have André the Giant armpits to get up to the bloody fire alarm on the ceiling.

Probably the low point was being banned from the swimming pool. Yes, this school had a swimming pool. A proper nice one as well.

Each team had an allocated hour slot to use the pool, so you all had to queue up and wait your turn. We were all in our little shorts, some of us in football shorts, while other teams were decked out in full swimming gear. I remember all the Yorkshire lads, who played for Harrogate, came out in goggles and all sorts, looking for a proper swim. Come on, lads, it's not the Olympics.

Most teams swam lengths and dived off the diving boards. As soon as we were allowed in, we were doing wrestling moves on each other: power bombs, suplexes, chokeslams – the lot. We were holding each other under the water to see how long we could last. There were a lot of frowns from those around us, but we didn't care. And then Storey decides to take it too far and grabs one of the Harrogate lads from the side and power bombs him in. I can still see the splash he caused.

JONNY STOREY: *I was only suplexing our lads!*

MARK WOOD: *No, you did it to that Harrogate lad, too. He almost drowned!*

STOREY: *That was when one of the officials came over and shouted at us. 'Where are your coaches?' Well, sir, do you see that green embankment over there, with the bloke with his top off, sunbathing? That's Stevie. As for the other one, he's around the corner with a tab on.*

WOOD: *Yeah, we got kicked out pretty sharpish. Ah well, at least Stevie got a bit of colour, and the sun would have helped his back, no doubt.*

★

Away days when you're younger are great fun. You go out together, spend time together and grow closer as a group. Now, it's probably not the most professional thing before a four-day game, to go out drinking. But certainly early on, the social side felt important. I still remember an away trip to play Worcestershire Under-17s we had. We stayed at the university and it just so happened that an Italian school exchange were also staying there. We were cracking on to the Italian girls, which was great fun but also comical. We were hanging out in the halls with these Italian lasses, trying to make conversation, holding up random objects and saying, 'plate'. 'Yes, plate'. 'Door'. 'Yes, door'. I remember walking away, thinking, 'Wow, I'm doing well here.' Idiot.

I used to think I was all right at languages. I took French at AS-Level. I used to love the lessons but then it came to the listening exam at the end of that year and I think I got the lowest mark the school has ever had. I remember the teacher telling us that but how I didn't have to worry because I could resit it the next year. I decided to bin it. It was such a step up. It went from GCSE where it was like '*Aujourd'hui, je voudrais parler du sport en France*' (Today I would like to talk about sport in France) to something much more complicated at a million miles an hour.

At the back of that AS exam there was a fifteen-mark question asking about what the farmer in the audio was talking about. I listened and listened and listened to this tape recorder and, honestly, I still had no idea. The only word I picked up on was '*poulet*'. So for a fifteen-mark answer, the only word I wrote was 'chicken'.

My first trip overseas on my own came when I was eighteen. I was part of the Durham set-up and during the winter they would send young cricketers on placements to challenge them, learn new skills and get used to standing on their own two feet. It's a great idea and it's sad some counties have had to cut down on them because finances in English cricket haven't been great in recent years given the impact of Covid-19.

You can get sent to Asia to work on bowling spin or playing it, or to South Africa and Australia where you work on fast bowling on harder pitches. My first trip away was for a season of club cricket on the Gold Coast in Queensland, playing for Palm Beach Currumbin CC. I ended up going back there for three winters. Initially, though, the academy coach had to kick us onto the plane for that maiden voyage because I didn't want to leave home.

I needed it, not just the kick but that time in Australia. I felt like I developed as a person each time I came back, which I suppose is how a lot of people feel after getting into a brand-new environment. I do think situations like that can do you a lot of good. I never thought of myself at the time as someone who could mix well with people outside my usual circle. But by the end, I felt like I returned with a bit more about me. More confident, more aware. I don't know what it was over those months that helped. Maybe having to fend for myself a bit? Even though I was incredibly well looked after by the captain, Ryan Armstrong, and his family.

I lived in Army's mum's house, a beautiful place on the water, and I was lodging with another player who came over from the UK. She was so generous with her time, constantly making sure we were all right, cooking for us and cleaning, though I tried to do my bit with the washing-up. The only time I think she ever got annoyed with us was when we used to crank the air-conditioning to as low a temperature as possible because it used to get so bloody hot. It wasn't the most cost-effective way of keeping cool, but the weather was roasting all the time, especially for a boy from Ashington. We used to try and get it back to the normal temperature before she got home. She suspected we were up to something because she'd hear us running to and away from the thermostat when the door opened. If she didn't, she certainly did when the bill came through.

Army and I are good mates now. It wasn't the best first meeting: I bowled my first ball to him in practice and he cut me for six in front of point, over the car park. He probably thought, oh great, another chancer from England. He actually dropped me first game, so I ended up playing Second Grade. I took seven wickets, though, so was soon in the Firsts. Early on, we beat Broadbeach – Army was telling us how good they were and was building us up all week because they had some really good players, including this one bloke called 'Fitzy' who would always be the top runscorer in the competition. I got him out second ball.

What I loved about Army was that we got on so well despite being from literally opposite sides of the world. He would work ten- or fifteen-hour shifts at the local hospital and then chaperone us, basically. If we weren't training together, we were watching the film *Step Brothers* over and over again and then just quoting lines at each other, which we still do to this day.

There was always room for activities at his house, where I'd go regularly to make Skype calls to people back home. His daughter was two at the time and I'd babysit every now and again. I even helped him with his assignments for the postgraduate degree he was doing. I like typing, so he'd handwrite them and I'd knock them out on the computer. I'd like to think he enjoyed having me around, though probably questioned why he put up with me when I almost wrote off his car by knocking his mailbox over...

RYAN ARMSTRONG: *Wait there. Not just my mailbox – the neighbour's mailbox, too. He was around one night and I had a couple of beers so I wasn't going to drive him and said he may as well just take my car. I give him the keys, he walks out and then a few minutes later he's sheepishly walking back in. 'Army... I've done something.' It's a double-brick letter box that's now lying on the ground. So he's crashed my car and taken out a couple of sturdy mailboxes. I had to tell the neighbour, of course. For the next week our mailbox was just a bucket with tape strapped over it. But yeah, I had to go and buy two new mailboxes.*

MARK WOOD: *In my defence, he had this winding drive that I had to reverse out of.*

ARMSTRONG: *I still don't think he's paid me for it, but I do have one of his Test shirts he signed for me with 'Sorry for the mailbox' written on it.*

WOOD: *We got through that, though. I'd like to think it made our relationship stronger. I always make a note of seeing him and his family when I'm in Australia and it was great he was able to come to my wedding. He always said*

I'd make it and it meant a lot that he was there for my first Ashes Test at Cardiff in 2015. I introduced him as my Australian captain to Alastair Cook, my first Test captain, and they hit it off. Probably a bit too well, to be honest.

ARMSTRONG: *We bonded over how hard he is to captain. Cookie actually asked if it was always hard work getting him up to bowl a second spell. I looked at Woody and said, 'Come on, mate, you're playing for your country!' He's not got that issue now, mind.*

I should also clarify a couple of things. Firstly, that cut shot. It was pure luck and I couldn't repeat it ever again. And secondly – I didn't drop him! I was begging to get him in First Grade from the start because he was easily one of the quickest in the competition. Our coach at the time was Graham White, very professional, very hardnosed, and he insisted – rightly – that there were guys who'd done their preseason who deserved a crack instead of being dropped. He said, 'I don't care if he's played sixty Tests or Glenn McGrath – he has to go through Second Grade and earn his stripes.' Thankfully, he did that pretty quickly.

There were tough times during those early trips to Australia. I got incredibly homesick and yearned for me mam's cooking or just to be around my mates chatting rubbish. The hardest points were the times on my own. I ended up leaving a week early in that first year, missing the Grand Final, because I couldn't bear being away for longer.

I used to call people at home as often as I could, which wasn't easy given the time differences. There were a few times I got my sums wrong and was waking people up in the middle of the night just to say hello. In a time before WhatsApp, I was firing off text messages left, right and centre, with photos here and there, using every bit of data I could to follow what people were up to back home on Facebook.

You can't really put a price on those home comforts. Well, I can – the phone bill was about £400.

DEREK WOOD: *Excuse me – £469. Not that we were counting.*

ANGELA WOOD: *Honestly, I nearly laid an egg. How does anyone rack up that much on a phone bill? Especially when we were calling him!*

DEREK: *That was almost as bad as the GCSE deal we struck with him.*

ANGELA: *He was a bright kid, but we thought he needed an extra push. So we said we'd give him £50 for every A. He ended up getting six As, and one of them was an A*!*

DEREK: *Yep, that was bad business on our part.*

MARK WOOD: *Did they make that deal for my A-Levels, you ask? Absolutely not. Though I only got A, B, D so it wouldn't have set them back as much.*

Mam and Dad were so angry, they threatened to bring me home. From then on, I had to go to the petrol station to buy top-up vouchers and it's fair to say my phone activity reduced significantly now that it was coming out of my pocket. Now, it's on the ECB so my parents can relax.

Those trips to Australia really set off the travelling bug for me and I've always loved going back to Australia, even if it's a bit far. As soon as scientists sort out teleportation, I'd happily go back and forth in an instant to see my old clubmates and knock about the different cities. Hobart's one of the most beautiful places and not too big, which is perfect for me. And as tough as the Ashes can be in terms of atmosphere, the Aussies are generally pretty good when you're out and about.

I consider myself so lucky that cricket has led to me travelling regularly. In a way, embracing the travel and the places we go to can be a great way of dealing with the challenges cricket throws at you.

If you just stayed in your room all day, you'd be alone with your thoughts and you'd just disintegrate. Unfortunately, we can say that with some certainty as England cricketers, given how much international cricket we have played over the last two years while in bubbles, or what the ECB describe as 'safe living environments'. Whatever you call it, it hasn't been easy to be in those settings and then turn it on to play tough cricket. Some deal with it better than others but it takes a toll on everyone in a different way.

I developed a pretty sound quarantine routine that I fine-tuned with each tour. The trick is to break it down by using your three meals to split things up. Try and do some fitness in the morning just to get the endorphins going. Things to watch on TV are always handy, particularly if they are live events, like sport. That way you can map your days out and have something to look forward to, and you can even organize a watch-along with your other quarantine mates along the corridor. Television series, particularly long ones like *24*, are ideal. And there is no better eater of time than *Football Manager*. I got the latest version in October 2021 and, by the time I left Australia in February 2022, I had made it to the 2039 season with AFC Wimbledon. Oh, and always – *always* – have an afternoon bath. In fact, quarantine or not, have one. They are mint and can even double as a swimming pool. An Instagram video of this in India at the start of 2021 might be my most popular to date.

Thankfully, the world is slowly reopening, and going out and exploring is that little bit easier. Like everyone else, I've got a list of places I can't wait to get back to and experience. One of those is Raglan in New Zealand. Back in 2018, Mark Saxby, Liam Plunkett and I seemed to be the only three people who had no interest in golf. So, while the rest of the lads were off playing the most boring sport in the world, we embarked on what we dubbed 'The Three Musketeers Tour'. We went to the cinema, hung out at Raglan beach in a camper van and went around exploring the town. It was the happiest without family I've ever been on tour. That was the end of a really long stretch that winter. I arrived in Australia at the start of November 2017, played for the Lions, was part of the Ashes squad, the ODIs and Twenty20 tri-series against Australia and New Zealand and then the Test series in New Zealand, which finished at the start of April 2018. I was the only person who didn't go home in that time. And then I went to the Indian Premier League. I was away for something like seven or eight months!

Unfortunately, golf looks like being a fad the current red- and white-ball squads are going to stick with. I've never been on board with any team fads, past or present. For a while it was *Call Of Duty*, which I get to a point. There was an embarrassing stage when lads would hire sports cars and drive around in them, thinking they were cool and not at all like blokes going through an early midlife crisis. The worst, by some distance, was fishing.

It started innocently enough in New Zealand when a few of us went fishing off a pier in Dunedin. But of course, that was not enough. A few of the lads who took it too seriously – professional cricketers, hey? – decided they wanted to do a proper fishing trip. A group of us – Chris Silverwood, Stokesy, J-Roy, Jonny and, I'm ashamed to admit, me – got together and hired a boat with this sixty-year-old sea captain. He said he had been doing it for fifty or so years, since a boy. It was a bit worrying that he didn't wear a life jacket and couldn't swim, but you have to admire the bravery. Plus, he was still here, so he must know what he's doing.

At first, the boat dropped anchor near where the river meets the open sea. Guess who turns out to be really seasick? Of course, it's me. The captain gave me peppermint to sniff, a wristband to wear so I looked like Andy Murray and said it'll pass. As I'm starting to feel horrendously ill at the back of the boat, the lads say my line has caught something. I get up, gan to me line. The captain is talking it up, saying it's probably a barracuda and will likely be the best one we catch today. I'm attempting to pull it up and trying not to be violently sick at the same time. The fish hits the side of the boat and falls in the water and everyone starts laughing. At that point, I'm done and start begging everyone to get us back to the river where the water isn't as choppy. Eventually, they see how bad I am and we turn to head back.

Unfortunately, for the rest of the trip, that just meant catching seaweed and rocks at the bottom of the river, so now everyone is annoyed with me. They all want to go back but I'm adamant on staying put. Then J-Roy comes up to me and says seasickness is like chickenpox – once you get it the first time, you can't get it again. I still don't know why I believed him. Off we go back to the sea and within thirty seconds I'm green again, on all fours, spewing off the side. It's my fault for being so trusting, but it's a mistake I'll never make again. I feel like I've said that a lot in this book.

PHIL SCOTT: *The great thing is he isn't into video games, he doesn't drink and he doesn't like coffee, so it makes him find different things, like crazy golf or general exploring. Which is good for me and anyone else who joins him.*

During the 2021/22 Australia tour, I was pottering about on my own and I get a call from him saying 'I can't do this, I can't just sit in my room – let's go and explore and see what we can fin''. We went to this national park just outside of Brisbane called Mount Coot-Tha. It was a couple of days after the Test where he bowled a lot, which just so happens to be when your muscles are at their sorest. We didn't quite plan the route so we went on a loop. At points he had to walk downhill backwards because his quads were in so much pain.

MARK WOOD: *Yeah that was an error, on my part. It wasn't quite a moonwalk, which might have made the whole thing look a bit cooler. I thought I'd get some sympathy from the strength and conditioning coach, but Phil spent most of the time filming me.*

Touring the Caribbean is probably the team's favourite. We've not got a great record there but you can't beat it for the beaches and vibe. Considering how much we play the West Indies, there are still islands we haven't been to as a team that I'd love to visit. I think because I'm a fast bowler and there's such a rich history of fast bowlers from the region, they always seem to talk us up. I'll always have fond memories of the place, given it was where I first felt properly at home in a white England shirt.

Personally, I think South Africa is my favourite country to tour. And no, not just because I took my second five-wicket haul there. Every city is different. Cape Town feels quite cosmopolitan with a lot going on, a bit touristy with a lot of surfer dudes. Then there are places like Johannesburg and Pretoria, which are totally different: a bit of edge to them and more aggressive towards you. Not in a way that they're going to beat you up, but you always seem to have big Afrikaans lads talking about how much stronger than you they are. Which was fine when we had a few Afrikaans lads of our own to go back at them, but it can be quite intimidating. All the grounds you play at are loud and compact. It feels like their fans are always at you, even in the hotels and restaurants. Johannesburg as a ground is pretty intense. To get on and off the field, you go down this walkway that is basically like the travelator in *Gladiators* encased in a Perspex tunnel. When you walk out to bat, the locals bang on it constantly to intimidate you, which can be pretty annoying if you're on the way back up after scoring nowt.

I've spent a lot of time in Potchefstroom, which is a city in the North West Province of South Africa. It's not the most happening place in the world, but we are often there for fast bowling and Lions tours. I'm beginning to think the ECB might have a loyalty card there or something.

Jokes aside, they have state-of-the-art sporting facilities there, which are great to use but can be slightly daunting when you're in the gym or on the running track next to genuine Olympians. It was quite humbling. The closest I got to getting the better of one of them was when I scared British Olympic gold medallist Christine Ohuruogu by jumping out of a wheelie bin.

One of the most memorable trips to Potchefstroom came on an England Lions tour there at the start of 2015. We had a strong group with us, some with international caps already, others who would go on to get them. Being all about the same age, it was a really sociable group and on one of our free days we decided to explore a bit. We came across this huge field where there seemed to be a huge festival going on. There was live music, bars and seemingly 30,000 people all having a whale of a time. Naturally, being in our early twenties, we figured we should have a look-see.

Myself, Jonny, Stokesy, Pudsy, Boyd Rankin, left-arm spinner Stephen Parry, who represented England in the 2014 World T20, and England Lions seamer Jack Brooks went over and decided to get a drink. Unfortunately, the bar closest to the entrance was rammed. Collectively, we thought our best bet would be the bar on the other side, which from a distance seemed to be quieter. The only trouble was the 30,000-strong crowd we had to get through. Ah well, it's probably worth it. We started walking through the crowd in single file: Pudsy, Jonny and Stokesy at the front, me in the middle, followed by Boyd, Parry and Brooks.

As we were walking through, I clocked these lads giving Jonny and Stokesy a bit of a funny look. By then, they'd both played a fair amount of international cricket and, both being ginger, probably stuck out more than the rest of us. I decide to put my head down and carry on walking. As I pick my head back up, one of the lads has pulled his arm back so far, like a slingshot, and crunched Stokesy in the neck. This lad, I should add, was absolutely massive. As were his mates. Maybe they recognized Stokesy, or maybe they just decided to pick on them because he's a big lad, but it made a horrible whack noise just beneath his jaw.

Pudsy and Jonny were slightly further ahead and hadn't realized something had happened so continued walking on. The next person on the scene is me. So there's me, Stokesy and four massive – *massive* – lads, all stood with their fists by their side. It was so bizarre. Stokesy asked, quite rightly, 'What the fuck do you think you're doing?' They didn't say anything, just stood there with their arms by their side, fists clenched, staring. I don't know how he wore that punch. That would have killed me. Stokesy looked at me and I just said to him, 'Let's just go.' He was incredibly calm in the situation. He'd probably done the odds and figured we wouldn't fare well in this bout. I'm hardly going to be first choice for a tag-team partner in any case.

A few seconds later, Boyd Rankin shows up, the biggest lad we've got, and goes, 'What's the matter, Stokesy, have you been pushed?' No, Boyd, he's been punched in the neck, mate. We all regrouped at the other bar and filled everyone in. I tried to tell people I was ready to throw down, introduce them to my fists, but no one was buying it. In the end, we moved on while the lads kept staring at us and finally made it to the other end of the field.

★

Without a doubt the most uncomfortable part of touring places like South Africa and India is seeing the poverty and homelessness right there in front of you. It's not a problem unique to those two countries: even at home in England, it seems to be getting worse. It's sad that people go through that. When I think back to Ashington and how people try and help each other out, it's hard to knock about in these privileged hotels while people are struggling right outside. When you get on the bus and you see how fanatical the fans are in some of these places then when you drive past and see people sleeping on the streets you realize how little some of them have. They've got nowt. It's awful.

Places like India and Sri Lanka were probably the biggest cultural shocks to me, mainly because of how we are treated. We're always treated well wherever we go, but in Asia there is so much glitz and glam around us. These are cricket-mad places and they love their cricketers, regardless of who they play for. They almost love us too much.

My introduction to the Indian Premier League in 2018 was such a shock to the system. I'd been to India previously at the age of twenty as part of a Durham development trip to Pune.

GRAHAM CLARK: *We were quite young and there was a lot of downtime in India. It was me, Woody, Paul Coughlin, who still plays for Durham, and Cole Pearce, who is now a coach at Durham. And after four days, you could see Woody wasn't good with the boredom.*

MARK WOOD: *I mean, we couldn't go out and it was a new place. So I was understandably stir crazy.*

CLARK: *Especially this one occasion when you got knocked out of a card game early.*

WOOD: *The Indian barber story?*

CLARK: *Afraid so. You could see Woody's mind ticking. He ended up getting his beard trimmer out and shaved a big chunk out of Cole Pearce's hair. Luckily, Cole, 15 at the time, was very young and naïve so he just laughed it off.*

But we thought we'd try and sort it out only for Woody to take the mickey again.

WOOD: *I shaved the back and sides and left him with a bowl cut.*

CLARK: *He kept it for two or three days and eventually we told him it was shocking and shaved his whole head, again with Woody's beard trimmer. Beyond fearing Cole might get seriously burned in the Indian heat because he was one of the palest blokes I know, we didn't think anything of it. Until we got to Newcastle airport, when Cole's mam was there waiting to pick him up. The look of horror when she saw his head and how we'd butchered it...*

WOOD: *I can still see it now. She was absolutely mortified.*

CLARK: *We were laughing at her reaction and saying, 'Ah, it'll grow back'. And she went, 'Yeah it will – but it won't grow back in time for his grandad's funeral tomorrow'. Woody's face dropped.*

WOOD: *I had to leg it out of the airport.*

When I went back to India as an overseas signing for Chennai Super Kings, it knocked my socks off. They were treating us like some kind of movie star, almost like I was a god. It was pretty unsettling because, well, I'm nothing special. Sure, I play a bit of cricket, but am I really worthy of all that fame? I don't know. The more I've gone, the more I've gotten used to it. I don't know how MS Dhoni, Virat Kohli and Sachin Tendulkar before them deal with all that expectation and still perform as well as they do. They must have incredible mental strength to not let all that pressure get to them. Sometimes I look at Kohli and think, 'Cor, I'd hate to be you.' Don't get me wrong – I'd love to have his talent. But to have 1.4 billion people investing all their hopes in you? It blows my mind.

The other thing I struggled with at the IPL was the food. I basically lived off margherita pizzas for a month because I didn't want to have anything else. Some might say I'm a bit of a fussy eater.

CHRIS WOAKES: *In India, there's no one worse than you. If there's anything with a bit of spice, you kick off.*

MARK WOOD: *It's not that bad. Is it?*

WOAKES: *Think of all the places we go and all the amazing food we have access to... and you are against all of it. We can't go for sushi. We can't go for anything spicy. It's generally quite generic. Pizza. Margherita pizza. I'm so glad I'm not in your IPL team. Checking every little bit of food. Making all these requests to the chef. Honestly, I want to give you a slap. I still remember that time in Australia when you got your torch out to check if the chicken was cooked.*

WOOD: *I don't like eating in the dark!*

I'm probably not much fun to eat out with. And yes, I have this thing where I need to check if chicken is cooked. But that is pretty normal. Right?

SARAH WOOD: *He has this constant fear of getting food poisoning. He has to check if chicken is cooked every time. And I when I say every time, I mean if he gets a meal with chicken pieces, he cuts through every single piece and asks me to take a look!*

MARK WOOD: *I just like things done a certain way!*

JONNY STOREY: *He's difficult. He's so homegrown. He'll go to a restaurant, like a nice Italian, and he'll just have chicken and veg. Why? He'll point to things on the menu and say, 'Oh, do you think that'll be cooked right?' No, no, Woody – they'll just send it out half-cooked. They'll just ignore their own standards and hygiene. He's obsessed with the colour of meat. He's got this state-of-the-art barbecue and he just churns out burned beef burgers.*

I'd like to promise to get better with that, but the truth is I'm just set in my ways when it comes to food. I'm going to blame it on being spoiled by me mam's cooking. But I'd like to think I'm much more open-minded about the world and travel as a whole, beyond the eating. At the time of writing, there are still places I haven't played, like Pakistan. I was gutted when our tour was called off in

October 2021 but was glad it got rescheduled a year later. It seems mad that I haven't been to a place like that, where cricket is regarded so highly and they have a serious team to be proud of.

I really can't moan about any of this, really. I'm going to these places to play cricket. I never thought I'd play for Ashington first team, so representing England in all these different countries is wild. Yes, we're there to do a job, but it's important to strike a balance with that and learning about other cultures and embracing both. I can't wait to tell Harry about the places I've been to and take him with me for more adventures before he's old enough to go out into the world and have adventures of his own. He might have to get someone else to help with restaurant recommendations, mind.

6

HOW TO STAY HEALTHY

There's a saying about experience that is relevant to anxiety. You never know you have it until after you get it. Then you realize all the moments that set you on this path were just that. Experience of anxiety.

I've now had five operations – three on my ankle, one on my left knee and one on my right elbow – which is a lot for most people, and I was overly nervous before every single one. I didn't like being cut open, didn't like the idea of having something seriously wrong with me. What if the issue is bigger than they think and I can't bowl again? Do I need to stop playing for my health? All those bad things that go through your head in that situation.

At the time, I tried not to think too much about those feelings. After all, it's not nice going for an operation so I figured that was causing all my stress. But on my way to my third operation, I was rooted to my seat on a flight that had just landed in Amsterdam, wondering if I was having a heart attack.

It was just before England's tour to Bangladesh in the winter of 2016. A few weeks earlier I had bowled my heart out for Durham to beat Surrey to stay up in Division One.

It turns out I was bowling on a broken ankle. I got Kumar Sangakkara out for a duck in the second innings, which was a big deal considering Surrey were chasing 281 for the win, he's a legend of the game and I had half a leg. It was torture, really, just trying to get through it. I was chuffed I did get through and that we won by 21 runs. Then the ECB decided to relegate us anyway.

The week after, it was clear I couldn't move my ankle even after I'd iced it. So I had to go and see a specialist surgeon in Amsterdam. He'd done Freddie Flintoff's ankle, Cristiano Ronaldo's ankle. My previous operations had been done by another guy, James Calder. He'd been brilliant with us: always left me full of confidence and stronger coming out of the operating room. But the ECB wanted me to see this other guy to ensure there was nothing more sinister going on with my ankle.

The trip hadn't started great. The ECB couldn't get us a flight out of Newcastle, my usual departure airport, so I had to go to Tees Valley Airport, which is an hour and twenty away. My SatNav took me to the back of the airport. It didn't help either that I was exhausted because hadn't slept a wink the night before through nerves. I still don't know how I made that flight.

As I sit down before take-off, my heart is racing, like it's about to burst through my shirt. This was around the time James Taylor had his heart problems. So I'm sitting there thinking, 'Oh no – is this what Titch felt like?'

During the flight, I twigged something was up because I couldn't get out of my seat. My legs were so shaky and weak. Like they were so heavy. My body felt like I had no energy, as if I was hypoglycaemic. I had pins and needles up my arms. I'm not the best flyer anyway, but I was losing it.

Now I know all those things are symptoms of anxiety. But when you don't know, you just panic. All those things put together, I must be having a heart attack. I started to sweat buckets. I'm just catastrophizing everything. When you are having a panic attack, a million things are coming through your head. So you say to yourself, 'Just breathe,' and obviously that's when you start to have trouble breathing.

When we landed, I realized I'd have to say something. Tell someone. Anyone. I was quite near the front and I just had to let everyone else off. I thought about telling one of the air stewards but I couldn't bring myself to do it. So I rang me dad.

'Dad, there's something wrong with me. My heart's pounding, my chest is tight, I can't breathe, I can't get up. What's up with me?!'

★

For a while I saw asking for help as a sign of weakness. I know I have something in my personality that says, 'Don't be soft, don't let people think you're soft, don't act soft.' Sometimes that's good, certainly in sport where you always want to give your best, and not show pain to your opponent. I think that insecurity of 'don't be soft' is ingrained in us, which didn't help when I was worrying about what was wrong during these panic attacks. It's like two sides of me were fighting each other. It took a while to understand that to admit I was struggling wasn't a bad thing.

Before, I'd mask struggle with humour and act like I wasn't bothered. I wonder how much of it was because of the area I grew up in. People around here would say, 'Ha-way man, you're from Ashington!' That you've got to be tougher because you've grown up hard. Maybe it was because I was small growing up? Maybe I felt I had to prove I was still tough and never take a backward step?

I didn't see it as a sign of weakness in anybody else. It doesn't make us any less of a cricketer or a bloke. I'm still trying my best to do well for me, for England, for my family. I'm still trying everything I can. By growing up in the environment I did, it's improved my cricket. But the cost of that was seeing any kind of pain as a weakness and trying to cover it up. I now only judge myself on a few things. If I have a bad day, or if I have a good day, the lows aren't super low and my highs aren't super high.

Now I'd openly say how I felt or what bothered us. It's taken a while to get to that point. And I still remember that moment sat on that plane when I reached out to my dad. My parents have always been there for us. Never have I felt I couldn't talk to them when I was struggling. This was just a new kind of struggle.

DEREK WOOD: *I knew he wouldn't call for just anything. To be honest, it was just about chatting very calmly to him. Trying to keep him level-headed around it all. Proportionate and balanced. It was just talking him through, telling him he'll get through this. You don't have to beat yourself up that you're feeling this way. It's not a weakness. You've admitted you're feeling like that and now we can help you. That is a show of bravery. To be honest, his mam has been the rock for him.*

ANGELA WOOD: *I usually sit up through the night. Especially when he was feeling the effects of his panic attacks. I'd always keep awake on the other end of the phone. If he wanted to text, he could text. I'd sit up and stay awake all night. I'd had experience before. The first time we saw Dr Calder, we travelled down on the train. When he came out, Dr Calder said his heart rate had got so high they were worried about it. When he got into the bay, every time a nurse came in to take his blood pressure, it would go sky high again. I sat there to 1.20 a.m. I tried to sneak out but it was a right heavy fire door. I went to the hotel, opposite the hospital. He rang at 3.40 a.m. to ask when I was coming back! But I'll always be there for him. Whatever, wherever.*

I don't think I'd be anywhere without my parents. The sacrifices they made when I was younger, and even as I've gotten older, when you probably think you don't need your parents as much. I'm much stronger now and feel like nothing phases us.

ANGELA: *Has he mentioned his fear of needles? The thing about it is—*

MARK WOOD: *Mam, not now. Not here.*

ANGELA: *—it stemmed from when he was a kid. He had his first injection and hated that doctor from then on. He used to always say: 'I don't like that Dr Needle Man because he made my leg bleed.'*

Cheers, Mam. Virat Kohli, Babar Azam and Steve Smith are probably reading this, thinking, 'Yeah, there we go, just mention Dr Needle Man and he'll be a right state.'

It's true. I hate needles. You'd think with the number of times I've been prised open (by qualified professionals, I should add) that I'd be used to a jab every now and again. No chance. Each one strikes the fear in me. I've left many a hospital, physio bed and hotel sofa drenched in my sweat after receiving one. There are probably Voodoo dolls around who would wince at the number of times I've been pricked.

The ECB has this app that tracks your injuries on the silhouette of a body. Mine is covered in red dots. It looks like the boardgame *Operation*. I wouldn't be able to tell you how many injections I have had off the top of my head. But I can tell you the worst because it was not just the most painful but a grave act of betrayal.

The national lead physiotherapist at the time, Ben Langley (a friend, or so I thought), called me up one day and said I needed to get something called a 'sugar injection' on my left ankle. Langers said it was just like a cortisone injection: quick jab and you're in and out in two minutes.

It turns out it's not like a cortisone injection – at all! They shred your ligament by rubbing the needle on it and then put sugar on it so it inflames. It encourages scarring and stiffening of the ligament. It was by far the worst thing I've ever had done. It felt like a burning sensation. I was nearly passing out. I told the guy, look, if you don't stop here, I am in serious trouble. Somehow, I got through it and called Langers after. All I could hear was laughter from the other end of the line.

That act of treachery aside, Langers has been a great ally. Without him, I'd never have been able to play for England. He was the one at the very start who invested time in me to get me physically right and continues to help me manage my ankle. He even introduced us to acupuncture, which is some going considering. But he's a nice Needle Man.

I first worked with him on a 2014 fast-bowling camp in Potchefstroom in South Africa. I wasn't playing for England at this point but was on their radar. I'd had ankle trouble but it wasn't keeping me out of action. It was just that, while my first spell would be quick, the next spells were not so. Essentially, Langers spent two to three months rubbing my ankle constantly.

He invested so much time and effort in me: he'd travel up to my home from his home in Worcester. He also invested in me as a person, and I really felt like I'd gained that level of trust. So, when it got to these operations and stuff, I could then go to Langers and it made it a lot easier. He basically got my ankle to a point where I could bowl consistently quicker and it wasn't keeping us off the park. Now our current England physio Craig De Weymarn is helping carry on that work.

Langers wasn't just a physio, he was someone I could lean on if I had troubles and doubts. So he was also a bit of a psychologist as well. He's since become a good friend.

That trust was vital for us to get my body in a good position, and I think it shows how much that human touch makes a big difference. Not in a literal sense, though I reckon since I started playing for England, I've had more physical contact with Langers than Sarah. But just being someone I could talk to, someone I could even share my fears with beyond what was hurting me physically at the time, continues to be a blessing. I could relate to him – his background, the way he was as a person. The fact that he cared.

He went out of his way to help me more than anyone else. He's a great listener. I'd say things and he wouldn't just treat me as a clinical subject, he'd listen to what I'd say and be quite emotive and treat me at the same time. He's not just a physio and he's not just telling you to make you feel good. If he wasn't around when I was coming through, I wouldn't be where I am today.

BEN LANGLEY: *I first met you back when Kevin Shine was running the pace programme. Kevin would mention players he had his eye on who he might take on the programme in the winter. I'd have to go and see them to make my initial assessments. Some of them would make the trip to focus on cricket development, some because of physical development in terms of strength and conditioning, and others might have injury issues that needed management.*

MARK WOOD: *I needed all of them.*

LANGLEY: *Yeah, you were definitely a remedial case! Once we started to work with one another, we had challenges with his ankle that's required surgery and we've had three operations on that, and they came at frustrating times. As your cricket would take another step up, you'd be hit by another challenge with the ankle. It got to a point where you and I worked quite intuitively with this ankle, because you felt like I understood what you were talking about.*

WOOD: *You've got iron thumbs, too. That helps. You would be on us for hours, rubbing the tendon to get rid of some scar tissue, say it was 'gritty' or 'thickened', rather than saying it was a bit stiff and tight. Using that kind of* *language helped us build a picture of what he was doing and what my problems were. The other thing is sometimes the physio and doctor are a lovely go-between for a coach and a player because they can get both sides. If it's just the coach pushing you to play or asking you how it is, you've always got them to help your side. That's something Langers has always backed me up in the past where I've not been quite right to play but I've been desperate to play, and he's stood up for us and said, 'Hold on – if you want him like this, he's not right.' You stopped me from making things worse but also made it not seem I was cowering away. That's another part of your personality that I love – you always had my back.*

LANGLEY: *You get coaches who want a black-and-white answer, and sometimes it's not. I think I've got a good ability to read when someone, if they have a problem, I'll know if it's because they've been slack. With you, I always appreciated that you were doing as much as you can. We just had to find something. Sometimes if a physio or doctor doesn't know, they'll just say keep with the programme, we'll get there eventually. But I'm not that sort of person. Even if the answer can be pretty simple, just things like massage or doing things a bit different, I don't like giving up.*

WOOD: *You can probably say Langers knows my ankle better than his own family.*

LANGLEY: *It's my fourth child.*

Injuries in sport are occupational hazards, and my ankle is no different. As a fast bowler, you're twisting your body every delivery and putting insane amounts of pressure through your bones. At the ECB centre of excellence in Loughborough, they do these tests with pressure mats to see how much stress you're putting through your foot. It turns out I put over seven times my bodyweight through my left foot – my landing foot, just before I release the ball – every time I bowl. Now, I know there isn't much weight to me, but seven times? It's no surprise my ankles ache.

Every fast bowler – heck, every bowler going – has niggles they are constantly dealing with. Recovery is a huge deal, especially with ice machines and massages. The schedule is so packed. There's always more cricket around the corner, so you've got to make sure you don't cut corners on any of it.

Even then, you need to so many measures in place to get you through games: the right boots, the right insoles, the right forms of strapping. Occasionally the right injection. They all feed into each other, so when you try something new, it has a knock-on effect to the others.

One of the weirdest developments through it was realizing I was allergic to a type of strapping. It turns out the stickiest tape contains zinc oxide. When it makes contact with my skin it starts to flare up. I'm not as allergic to it as Ben Foakes, mind, whose skin looks like you've poured acid on it when he gets some of that on him. It's like a third-degree burn.

Because of how tight my ankle gets strapped, I'm often left with cuts across my achilles. To me, that's just a bit of collateral to get through a big game. I actually don't mind it – it makes us feel like a Spartan warrior. I'm just trying to keep up with Stokesy in terms of being tough. Though I'm not going to win that battle.

When Stokesy broke his wrist punching that locker in the Caribbean after getting out for a first-ball duck against the West Indies, he went for an operation to get it fixed. The doctor gave him two choices: a general anaesthetic to knock him out completely while they operated, or a local so that he was still awake and they'd just numb his arm. The catch was that with local he'd be able to leave the hospital quicker, so Stokesy took that option. About halfway through the operation, Langers noticed he was grimacing and asked him if he could feel it. 'A bit.' Finally, Stokesy admitted to being in some kind of discomfort, and all it took was someone drilling a hole through a bone.

A lot of working out the right precautions or managing pain is trial and error – finding out what works and what doesn't. If I'm honest, some of that error has come from my own clumsiness.

One time on holiday I was just running through a field without a care in the world and accidentally stepped on a plank of wood that had rusty nails sticking through it. One of them pierced my foot and I was in absolute agony. The tetanus jab that followed was just as bad. Then there was the time I thought I'd do a good deed for Army's mam when I was staying with her during my time with Palm Beach. She looked after us during the day then worked nights so, as a treat, I thought I'd mow the grass so she could wake up to a nice pristine lawn. She had one of these mowers with a pull-string engine and it was a temperamental little thing.

After a few frustrating yanks, I decide to pull it as hard as I can. As I've done so, it's lifted off the floor, started and then come straight down on my foot, taking all the skin off my big toe. Another inch down and it would have taken my big toe off my bowling foot completely off. My screaming must have woken Army's mam up – so much for doing her a favour.

RYAN ARMSTRONG: *He's sensationalized it a little bit. I work in a hospital and I got a call from him. 'Army – I've got to come in. I've been mowing your mam's lawn and I've run over me foot!' I thought he was missing a toe, then he came in and it was just this little nick. He played that weekend!*

To think, that would have been the end of my career then and there. Imagine how often I'd fall over in my bowling action then? Come to think of it, maybe I'd have got a bionic toe and bowl quicker while never falling over? Was that an opportunity missed?

Probably the stupidest misjudgement on my part came in the summer of 2017. I had these specially made insoles for my left boot, which helped cushion my landing and made sure the impact was distributed evenly. I wore them during the Champions Trophy and they worked brilliantly. After we lost to eventual winners Pakistan in the semi-finals, I got rid of those boots without taking the insoles out.

When it came to the South Africa Tests later that summer, I realized my error but figured the old ones would do the trick while I waited to get another pair of the newer versions. Safe to say they didn't. I really felt the pain in the first innings and it just got worse, and as a result I could only bowl one over in the second. I should have sat out of the next Test, at Trent Bridge, but when Rooty asked us if I was fit enough to play, I said yes. I had my new insoles so figured all would be fine, that I could grit my teeth and play. But I didn't perform well at all. The damage had already been done.

That attitude ended up doing more harm to me than good. I dropped out of the XI and didn't play a Test in that winter's Ashes. I wish I had made a different decision: firstly not to throw away those insoles and secondly not to say yes at Trent Bridge. Who knows how long it cost me in terms of feeling more settled in the Test side?

It wasn't the first time I said yes to playing when I wasn't ready. I'd like to think I'm more sensible around that kind of stuff now. Because it's not just about doing yourself damage, but you're hurting the team as well by not being as good as you could be. Sometimes, yes, you can take the pain and get through it, especially if getting through is for the good of the team.

A good example of both came during the 2019 World Cup final. I twanged my groin in the second over, trying to stop myself from falling over as I do in my follow-through. I usually just let myself tumble because when you're running in that quick, trying to stop can do yourself more damage. But because it's Lord's, because it's a final, because it's the biggest game I've ever played in, I tried to not look a tit. And I ended up stumbling instead of falling and straining my groin.

Immediately all sorts are running through my head as I'm walking back to my mark. I realized I could not let it bother us. Folk already think I'm held together by Sellotape – I don't need this in a World Cup final. I manage to get out of that first spell with Ross Taylor trapped LBW: getting a few away from him before nipping the ball back in at his back leg. I think that's the worst of it. Then, of course, I do my side.

Doing your side is funny. Well, it's not that funny – it feels like someone's poking a hot electric rod into your side. But it's the kind of pain you think has gone after it happens, and then you start to breathe and realize it's still there. I did it in the 45th over of the innings. I've pulled down my left arm for a quick bouncer and felt the right side go. The next delivery was to Tom Latham who was going well. He'd hit me for six two balls earlier and I had two balls left. Morgy comes up to us and I wonder if I should tell him. It felt a bit like admitting to your parents that you've crashed the car.

'What's your plan here?' Morgan asked. I decide to be honest.

'I think my side's gone.'

'Riiiight…' he said, looking at me. 'What do you want to do? Can you get through it?'

'I think so,' I said.

'Right, OK. No problem!' And then he just waltzes back to his mark. That was him in a nutshell right there – chilled and with every faith in us.

I bowled that ball and I remember thinking to myself, 'This is bad here.' I walked back to my mark and kept touching it and grimacing. Then I realized they were showing my face on the big screen. People always say they can tell when I'm down because of my body language on the field. I don't think of myself as an emotional guy, but I do care about a lot of things. Maybe that's the same thing. I think I have my feelings in check, sometimes to a fault. But I am probably quite hard on myself for things that are beyond my control.

In that situation I couldn't make it obvious. I didn't want New Zealand lads to know I was struggling. I didn't want the other lads to know I was struggling. And I didn't want the crowd to know I was struggling. So I started trying not to touch it and puff out my chest. I tried to do this thing where I look at the tops of the stands so I didn't have my head down looking miserable. Promoting good body language, they say. I got to my mark and just thought, 'Right, don't let anyone down here. They are only 211 for 5 here with five overs to go after this delivery.' The side was obviously done. In that moment I knew I was out of the Ireland Test and, probably, out of the whole Ashes. 'Give this everything you've got,' I told myself, 'and deal with the consequences later. This is the most important delivery you're ever going to bowl.' My last ball of 2019 was a 92 mph bouncer.

I'd got through my ten overs with the ball but I didn't want to get off the field. I was probably a bit too proud, but I also felt bad if one of the twelfth men had to come on st few overs. I then ran for a ball at midwicket I was in no fit state to field. Morgy and Rooty ting at us to get off and they were right. I had to I knew that too. And it was only when I started walking off that I realized why I didn't want to leave.

Whether you've had a good time in the field or a bad one, walking off with your teammates is a comforting feeling. Whatever has just happened, you have done it together. But walking alone towards the boundary and then through the pavilion, while the rest of your team is still out there, carries a real sense of shame. A feeling I've had so many times before. A mixture of embarrassment and disappointment. That your body has let you down again. That you are walking through the Long Room during a World Cup final when you haven't finished the job. That you are leaving your mates out there.

The overriding emotion should be about my bowling. I bowled OK, not great, for 1 for 49 from my ten overs. I should have bowled miles better, but it was not so bad. But I was knackered again. The last eight weeks had been incredible. To get through all those games at that intensity was something to be proud of. And I needed a bit of distance to look at the World Cup final and think, well, is it really that surprising after trying to bowl 95 mph every other ball that something eventually went after ten games? I'm proud now, but I was gutted then.

★

Athletes always have a base level of self-esteem point you've got to think you're better than a large of people to be good enough at something to get paid well, travel the world and represent your country. People carry it in different ways and in cricket, because it's such a mentally taxing game, you get the full spectrum.

Some cricketers are just beaming in confidence. I remember when MS Dhoni used to walk out to bat, he looked so calm, so assured. No matter the score or the situation, or if he was on a bad run of form, he'd always look like he was walking into his own house. Even off the field, he's got the demeanour and magnetism of a movie star.

When I played under him at Chennai Super Kings in 2018, it was incredible to see what he was like up close. There was a game we played away to Royal Challengers Bangalore. The game was dead and buried but he just belted New Zealand's Corey Anderson all over to win it for us. I was sat on the side, watching with Shane Watson, Faf du Plessis and David Willey. Watson said, 'Watch, we'll still win here.' I wasn't having any of it, they should easily win from here. But Dhoni waited and waited until the end and just went bang. He finished with 70 off 34 balls to chase down a target of 206!

We used to travel by plane for all our games. Dhoni would always sit with us in economy even though he obviously could have sat in business class with some of the other CSK management. Always with his family, too. He'd travel in shin-high combat boots, camouflage army trousers, bright Chennai top, aviators and this commando cap. He looked like something out of a *Top Gun* film. It was like he was an undercover marshal. If anything went down, he'd be the guy saving the day at the end of the film. Not only was he a gun wicketkeeper batsman but also an action hero.

He had this guy who used to travel around with him called Khalil who would always look after his bags.

Whenever they went through the detectors, he'd go over and say, completely straight-faced, 'This is Dhoni's bag.' All of a sudden, the customs officers could not have been more helpful. There was an unfounded but (for the benefit of any libel lawyers reading this) no doubt this was rumour flying around the lads that he carried a firearm with him at all times, them taking advantage of me being the most gullible person in the world.

Dhoni would often have us around to his room to hang out, watch football or just chat. There'd be a few of us there, Dwayne Bravo, Harbhajan Singh – these other superstars in their own right. And they'd be hanging on his every word, or cracking a joke to see if he'd laugh. He just had everyone around him under his spell. I used to go back to my room and call my mates and be like, 'Mate, I was just in Dhoni's room hanging out. How mad is that?!'

I was pretty much on the other end of that scale. I knew I was capable, like, and I feel like everywhere I've got to in cricket has been on merit. But I felt like I had to fight for everything. And I always needed encouragement to know I was doing the right things, whether through wickets or praise.

Generally, I'd say that's a healthy way to be. If you fight for something, you're always more appreciative when you get it. And because you value it that little bit more, you work even harder to keep it. Growing up in Ashington, you had to graft for every bit you got. But you can then find yourself clutching for things just out of reach or squeezing things too tightly that you already have.

The trouble, I found, was those lulls when it felt like you were stood still. There were a few years early in my England career when I just wasn't producing what I knew I could. I couldn't understand why I'd go back to Durham and get wickets, but I'd come back for England and it just wouldn't happen.

It was sort of like I was trying too hard or I played games when I shouldn't have done. That didn't do my career any favours. I'd got back in the team and just played through injuries. It was stupid, when I think about it. It just cost me in the long run.

I'd start to get bitter, looking at other bowlers across the world and thinking, 'I'm as good as these guys, why is it not happening for *me*?'

Cricket's a bad sport for that – feeling hard done by. It's very easy to blame others or attribute your own bad performance to bad luck. The guy in club cricket who is never out LBW because it's always the umpire's fault. The guy in county cricket who's bitter because he didn't play for England. Sometimes, you have to look at why are people thinking like this, rather than just thinking they've got it wrong. Because naebody I've come across in, say, the England set-up, are pretentious for the sake of being pretentious. There's always a reason why. Ask yourself how you can get better. Of course, there are times when you can feel hard done by and hacked off. And definitely I've been as guilty as anyone for moping.

On the field, there were two chats I had, both in Sri Lanka in 2018, that set me on a better path. The first was with Trevor Bayliss after a practice in Pallekele. The ground is pretty amazing, forests all around and a climate to match. It's hot and sticky and you can end up losing a couple of kilos of moisture just in training alone.

That was a bit awkward because I didn't really want to confront him. He's the head coach who has got a lot more to worry about than just one lad who isn't really playing. Plus, our relationship was pretty straightforward: I would take the mickey out of him for being an Aussie, he'd take the mickey out of me for being 'Scottish', as he kept calling us. We'd just have a laugh together. I was the joker of the team and he'd love that about us. And I didn't really want that dynamic to change. Especially as I was sweating buckets at the time because of the heat as I go to speak to him in the changing room.

Trevor was a fantastic coach. He spoke really well, and when he spoke everybody listened. He carried respect, carried himself well. He spoke simply but the simplicity of him made it so good: clear messages cultivated a great atmosphere. Now I'm trying to be all quite serious: 'Why am I not in the team – Test and one-day? What do I need to do to get back?'

I was bracing myself for some technical chat: that I

needed to get better at slower balls, yorkers (for one-day) or consistent pace for Tests. Instead, he just says, 'Mate, I want to see a bit more mongrel from you. I want you to go away on that A tour, I want you to bowl quick in the nets, bounce people!' That wasn't something I really did. I didn't really want to be knocking my friends' heads off in the nets.

But I went away and did what he said and, ultimately, I got back in the team. That Lions tour later that year in Australia, I believed I was the best there, that I was an England player and people looked up to us. So when I went back to the England team, I carried that confidence on.

The second chat I had was with Jos at the end of that series, after we had won a one-day and a one-off Twenty20. We were all at the bar, celebrating what had been a brilliant month or so as a team, but I just couldn't get involved. I was propped up at the bar with Jos and decided to get some advice.

JOS BUTTLER: *I think I remember that. This is the thing with you, Woody, you don't drink so you just remember everything. It's pretty annoying.*

MARK WOOD: *Yeah, it was you and Morgy at the bar and I kind of just unloaded on you both. I was feeling particularly down and I said, 'Jos, what do you think I need to do with my game? Where do I need to get better? Rabada and Cummins get four wickets every ODI. I never do that.'*

BUTTLER: *I remember saying you're not realizing the wickets you are getting. At the time you were getting the best batters out in the opposition or breaking a big partnership. As opposed to looking at your own column, look at the effect you have on the game because you're getting the key wickets out. You've always had all the skills, and when you're completely fit, you unlock more and it challenges batters. You create good angles, use the crease well.*

WOOD: *It really meant a lot to us. Where I was thinking doom and gloom, he put a positive spin on it. I'd run through a brick wall for Morgy, but at the time I was thinking he didn't rate us any more. Maybe that's it. Maybe this is me done. But that chat with you both made us feel so much better. You both weren't just saying it from a colleague's point of view, you were saying it as friends. You being the wicketkeeper you get to see what I'm doing all the time.*

BUTTLER: *Yeah, I mean you've definitely kept me on my toes with that stupid 'jump wide' thing you do when you're changing the angle. That throws my alignment off. I see him jump, then I jump. It changes my whole wicket-keeping routine because I can't set too early because I've got to see where he bowls from.*

WOOD: *Little-known fact: we call Jos's gloves 'the vipers' because he's got the green gloves. And they gobble up* *everything. Do you remember when I used to sing, 'Jos Buttler, No Byes' to the tune of 'No Woman, No Cry'?*

BUTTLER: *I do. How times have changed, eh?*

It was from that point on I was more robust, physically and mentally. I felt comfortable in my own skin and trusted everything around me. The support from family and friends never went away, but now I felt like I had that same kind of support from my teammates, coaches and support staff. I stopped worrying as much about what other people were doing. It's an awful phrase, 'controlling the controllables', but this was the first time I had confidence that if I worked at things within my control, then I couldn't ask for anything more. I suppose you might call that satisfaction. Perhaps even 'peace'.

The rewards started to come: the five-wicket hauls, the World Cup win, the acceptance. People I respected were respecting me, and people who maybe thought I wasn't good enough were being won round. Defining yourself by those successes are never good because you end up crashing emotionally when those successes dry up. But I made sure to cherish each one's memories without letting those moments be the only fuel for my self-worth, if that makes sense? For now, the balls and stumps I've taken from games as mementos are at my parents' house.

I still remember the period after my third ankle operation in 2016 when I didn't want to leave the house. I remember this one drive to Wetherby, which is about two hours away. I had to pull over two or three times to calm myself down. Stuff like that had never happened before. How could it? I'm a happy-go-lucky person. I can go out and chat to people. I can drive two or three hours, no bother, singing my head off in the car. I used to get other cars pointing and laughing at me in traffic jams when I'm belting out songs. All that had gone. It was a time in my life that, because of the operations, my anxiety was at an all-time high.

To have that happiness back feels like the biggest thing worth celebrating. It didn't come easy. I worked with a psychologist, started using Headspace – this meditation app – to bring back the joy in all the things I used to love doing. Granted, I didn't see the relevance in any of that stuff at the time. But eventually I started understanding how my mind works a bit better and why this was happening.

Do I still suffer from anxiety? I'm not sure. I'd say 'no' but that I still get anxious. The thing that has changed is the negative internal talk. I stopped thinking: 'I shouldn't be feeling like this', 'why am I feeling like this?', 'this is weakness', 'why am I feeling bad, what is wrong with us?' I replaced them with positive thoughts, about how I could get back to being at the level I was before. Perhaps even better. I noticed that difference particularly after my elbow surgery. Having done well in the 2021/22 Ashes, I was disappointed to lose momentum with that injury that meant I could only bowl five overs on the third morning of the First Test in Antigua on the Caribbean tour that followed. At another time, I might have wallowed. But the experience of coming back those previous times gave me perspective. Funnily enough, I was glad it was a 'new' kind of injury. I'm a bit bored of having my ankle cut open. An operation at the end of March went well, aside from a video that went viral of me talking absolute gibberish while still feeling the effects of the anaesthetic. I was back bowling a month later.

I feel like I can cope with and talk about the physical and mental ordeals now because I understand them better. I think that began on the return flight from Amsterdam. Concerned about another episode, I picked up the in-flight magazine and every time I worried about my heart or my breathing or my operation, I read the same line I was on over and over again. I made it to three pages over the course of the seventy-five-minute flight, but that helped. Also, I remember watching *The Last Kingdom*, this historical fiction television series set loosely around Bamburgh Castle in Northumberland, and that really helped.

So, yeah, if you suffer with anxiety or injury don't be afraid to be open about it. And in the meantime, in-flight magazines and Anglo-Saxon warfare are great ways to take your mind off things.

7

HOW TO KEEP LEVEL

Are you all familiar with Lucas the Spider? No? Well, you've come to the right place.

Lucas is a spider who's got his own animated series, so he's kind of a big deal. He's a cute little thing: big eyes, eight little legs, a lovely outlook on life, always getting into some form of high jinks. He has become something of an obsession for my son Harry since he first clicked on one of his YouTube videos. They're only thirty seconds long, which is perfect for his attention span (and mine, to be fair). Spiders are now his favourite thing, along with diggers, with digging for spiders in the garden in the middle of that Venn diagram.

As it happens, Lucas – in toy form – spent the entire winter of 2021/22 on tour, all the way through the T20 World Cup and the Ashes. He contributed little with the ball or in the field, though I only did marginally better than him with the bat. However, he did lift my spirits across a gruelling five months on tour.

The reason Lucas was there in the first place is because the ECB had sorted it with the ICC that our families could come with us out to the UAE for the 2021 Twenty20 World

Cup. Given the Covid restrictions around the tournament, it was incredibly generous and something that a lot of us needed, especially those who had spent so much of the previous two years in bubbles.

Sarah and I decided that it was probably best if she and Harry didn't come over with me to Australia. At the time we had to make the decision, there was still a lot of uncertainty around living arrangements, even the venues for some of the Test matches. So when our World Cup came to an end, Sarah and Harry returned home, leaving behind a few odds and ends that included Harry's digger pyjamas and, of course, Lucas.

At every hotel across Australia, I'd lay his pyjamas out by the bed because they had his smell, which would comfort me before I went to sleep. And I made sure to put Lucas on display. Whenever I felt bad, I'd look at Lucas. It reminded us there's more to life than cricket. I'd think of Harry at home, knowing how happy he'd be to see us when I finally walk back in the door. I love playing for England. I'm proud of playing for England. But at those low moments, it's important to remember the world – your world – outside the game.

But at the end of the 2021 Melbourne Test, that didn't work. We'd lost in three days – two and a bit, if we're being honest – and, at 3–0 down after the first three matches, the Ashes were already gone. It was a sickening feeling. It felt like we were letting people down: supporters, teammates, ourselves and our families. When I eventually got back to my hotel room, I took one look at Lucas and felt horrific. Absolutely awful. I couldn't bear to look at those big eyes. I'd let him down. I'd let Harry down.

You hear a lot about athletes talking about how family, specifically kids, changes their perspective. I think that's true in any walk of life. Your family and friends keep you level. They stop you from getting too full of yourself and give you confidence when you need it most. They've been on the journey with you so know what you have had to go through to get where you are. And I suppose that means even when you're low, they can hit you with some hard truths. My parents are good like that. My dad sends me messages at the end of the day's play, telling me if I've bowled crap.

DEREK WOOD: *I don't quite put it like that!*

MARK WOOD: *He does.*

ANGELA WOOD: *Dad might say he's played crap. I always say, 'Well… I've seen you play better.' He shouldn't ask us if he doesn't want us to tell the truth!*

Anyway, the point is, spending time with people you know well who aren't necessarily in your field (pun absolutely intended) is good, and being able to tour with family is always a bonus. Probably not for them, mind, because the time you spend together isn't exactly perfect.

If you think about a Test match, that's five days you're out of action between eight in the morning and pretty much eight at night. Then there are the two practice days leading up to it, which either take the whole morning or the whole afternoon. So that's basically a full day split across two when you can spend time with them. Not to mention the fact that if you've got young kids who wake up during the night, you often sleep in adjoining rooms to ensure you're as fresh as possible during games. It's the partners who suffer most. I don't think I could ever repay Sarah for what she does when I'm gone. It's probably harder when she's on tour, because she deals with an excitable Harry during the day and then a tired, grumpy me at night.

That was why the T20 World Cup in 2021 was so unique – in a good way. Given the restrictions, all the team and families became one big family. We basically had Th8 resort, on Palm Jumeirah, to ourselves so the kids could roam about the place. The tournament coincided with Harry's birthday so we had a do there. David Willey dressed up as Spider-Man and, you know, was pretty good. He's very agile for a big bloke and was doing all the movements around the swimming pool. If they're looking for a replacement for Tom Holland, he certainly could do a job. I reckon if Spider-Man played cricket he'd be an all-rounder, too. Plus Willey's got the calves of a super hero already.

We also went big for Halloween, with a 'Trick or Treat' to every hotel room and a scavenger hunt sorted by

Tymal Mills's wife, India. A few of the players used it as an excuse to dress up, though we had to get resourceful. I dressed up as a mummy with rolls and rolls of tubigrip wrapped around us. It wasn't exactly a great leap for me, given how much strapping I usually wear.

The spirit in the group was great. A lot of us have played together for years, some have known each other for even longer and our families have grown close. It felt like the perfect balance of focus towards winning a first T20 tournament since 2010 and staying level. Then came the end and it was absolutely gutting.

Losing that semi-final to New Zealand as we did was painful. They were brilliant but we'd hardly put a foot wrong all tournament and I felt we showed people why we were favourites coming into it. But T20 is a volatile format and we were on the wrong end of it. I wasn't happy with my own performance. Because of injury, I played only two games at the tournament. I bowled average and we lost both.

The logistics around the trip to Australia meant we had to stay in the UAE and travel from there to Queensland. But our families had to leave, meaning we had five days on our own.

I didn't know what to do with myself. The days were usually so structured with cricket, playing diggers with Harry and smashing the hotel up a little bit. Then we'd go to the pool, build sandcastles, play 'shops' in the hotel lobby where he'd pick up expensive books and pretend he was buying all this stuff. He'd have his nap, Sarah and I would tidy up, then he'd be up again and we'd be back to the pool, onto a playground, then we'd go out and look at the moon because he loves the moon. Then back to the room and watch his favourite programme and he'd be off to bed. And then Sarah and I would finally relax. Then the next day would start all over again.

When they left, I think that was the saddest I've ever been, dropping them off at the airport and coming back to an empty room. A room that had been full of energy and noise was now just soulless. I've never felt so emotionally lost.

Usually after a loss like that, the best thing is to get away from the game. To go and visit a place you love to visit, do the things you love to do, be with the people who will take your mind off things. Do something that brings you joy. Which in this case was anything but cricket. Anything but reminding yourself of the pain you experience and the trophy that got away.

What is not recommended is, say, going to another pretty big series like the Ashes on the same plane as the Australia team who have just won the World Cup you wanted to win. If you were to design the worst-case scenario given how we were feeling, there it was. The last thing you want to do is be forced to spend time with a bitter rival in an enclosed space where they can rub their success in your face. There's a reason boxers don't share a car home after the fight.

Thankfully, the Aussies were on a different side of the plane and, to be fair to them, were pretty quiet. They were probably exhausted from all the celebrating they'd done the night before. Never mind, it's not like we didn't get a good look at them having the time of their lives over the months to come.

I think that might be the worst thing about cricket – how close you are to other teams' celebrations. As someone who bats down the order, I'm often there at the end when the opposition wins. Eleven blokes going crazy over a win right in front of your face? I wouldn't recommend it.

India at Lord's in 2021 was a sickener. We were in a great position to win after getting a first-innings lead. Then India's tail got runs in the second – Mohammed Shami and Jasprit Bumrah scored 89 between them and gave us a chase of 272, which we got nowhere near. Jimmy Anderson and I were batting together at the end and getting pelters from them in the field because we were up against it and there'd been bad blood throughout that game. It was horrible, to be honest. In fact, I don't think I've ever been in the middle when we've won a game with the bat.

I came close to helping us save a Test in October 2015 against Pakistan. We were trying to bat out the game for a draw, and Adil Rashid and I stuck together for 29.2 overs at the end. I got out with ten overs to go and then Rash got out with six overs to go. He'd batted brilliantly as well and ended up with 61. It was gutting.

I was the last man out when we lost to Sri Lanka in the group stages of the 2019 World Cup. That was hard. I believed I'd let everyone down because I'm definitely sure Stokesy would have hit the winning runs. He'd started chinning it and was on 82, and we only needed 21 more runs to win. It was awful. I know it's down to everybody, but I felt personally responsible because I felt if I stayed in and blocked one or two balls, then we'd win. Stokesy was whacking it. My thought process was really good: I spoke to Jos and the team analyst, Nathan Leamon, about the best way to bat against reverse swing. I'd planned to stay leg side a little bit to negate LBW. Then I edged Nuwan Pradeep behind because the ball held its line and we were all out. I felt horrendous as Sri Lanka went wild.

Cricket being the self-proclaimed 'gentleman's game' means you've got to grin and bear it. Shake hands, say well played, watch them lift a trophy or urn, and then slink off back to the changing rooms where you can wallow in private.

The atmosphere in a changing room that's just lost is enough to put you off losing altogether. Some people are packing away their kit diligently as a way to calm down. Some are in a rage, throwing stuff into their bags as quickly and loudly as possible. Some are still in their kit, sitting there just staring into the distance. It's as sombre and quiet as you'd expect, until the noise of the opposition celebrating all together in the other dressing room comes down the corridor. It's like being in a funeral while it's kicking off at the wedding next door.

Even though you're playing at the pinnacle of professional sport, there's only one thing you want to do at a time like that: comfort eat. That's probably universal when you're feeling that low, no matter what you do in life: sit on a couch, wrapped in blankets with something on the TV and just stuff your face. We don't, of course. Well, most of the time.

By the time we arrived in Australia for our quarantine at the Mercure on the Gold Coast, we were in such a bad place. It's hard to describe but, now that I think back, I was probably a little bit depressed. I was so down because of the way we'd lost to New Zealand. It's such a big downer. And over the course of the fourteen-day quarantine, left to our own thoughts, those feelings were only going to get worse.

When we got to our rooms, Cricket Australia had very kindly provided a care package of jelly sweets, chocolates, crisps, all kinds of snacks. Now, I don't know if it was a ploy, but every one of us smashed through it all and, let's just say, the hips didn't lie.

As part of our fitness testing, we do something called a 'skinfolds' test. You might have heard of it before, but basically it is a way of estimating body fat by pinching the skin on a few different areas of the body with callipers, and the readings are added together. My skinfolds are usually sound: the majority of the time I'm between 50 and 54 millimetres, and at one point I was as low as 46, which is probably too low. By the time I got out of quarantine, I was 65 – the highest I've ever been in my career! The others were the same: Jos had gone up by 13, Woakes up by 9 and Dawid Malan had gone up a whopping 20. We obviously got down to our usual levels before the First Test, and I think the management were a bit more understanding of those numbers given how the previous month had been.

I think empathy is something that really counts, especially among a squad. It's there when you celebrate team and individual success, but also when things aren't going well. Especially so when things aren't going well. It's easy enough being cheery and everyone's mate when things are good and you yourself are playing well. People were coming up to us in Australia, telling me how well I've bowled, both Aussie fans and former players. As nice as that is, it's not much of a boost when you're not winning and your teammates are going through a rough time.

PHIL SCOTT: *Dressing room environments can be really insecure, with people looking over their shoulders about their place or trying to work out where they stand in the team. There'll be thirty blokes in a room really trying to macho it up, not trying to give too much away. But the brilliant thing about Woody is he's comfortable giving compliments. If you are smartly dressed, if you do something nice or look good - he'll tell you. I still remember occasions things were quite tense one morning and he cut the tension simply by telling Jimmy Anderson he looked beautiful today. The room went quiet until a few people piped up, 'Actually, yeah, Jimmy - you do look great'. And that love started to flow. He brings the love and everyone goes with him.*

MARK WOOD: *With Jimmy it's usually, 'Wowza, yee look good!' Or I tell him he's got cracking hair or looks smart as a carrot. When does he look anything but?*

Tours are when that bond needs to be at its strongest, and England are a good group for that. The places we go to are amazing, but we're only human and not everyone deals with being away from home as well as they'd like, especially if you've had to leave your family. Little things can go a long way, whether that's going out for dinner together or even surprising someone with a taste of home every now and again. For me, those are Ferrero Rochers. Woakesy often gets us them and, I tell ya, there's nowt better than those little clouds of heaven to give you a boost.

CHRIS WOAKES: *To be fair to Woody, he returns the favour. He knows I love Chocolate Digestive biscuits and there has been a couple of times when we're in bubbles that he's knocked on my door and handed me a pack out of nowhere. It's those nice little moments when you're away that keep you ticking along. Of course, true athletes that we are, we don't eat them.*

MARK WOOD: *No, course not. You and I, we do spend a fair bit of time together on tour. We hang out and watch football in our rooms, chat rubbish, go for coffees...*

WOAKES: *Yeah but... it's a bit awkward at times because you're not a coffee drinker. Sometimes we'll be at this nice joint and you'll just get a juice. I didn't have my family out with me in Australia, but I felt like I had my kids sitting with me when sat with you.*

All right – cheers, Woakesy! He and I, along with Stuart Broad and James Anderson, were our own little group of singletons out on the last Australia tour. We hung around, had a few scooter rides around Brisbane and generally checked in on each other. As bowlers, that help extended into training as well. One of the best when it comes to that kind of thing is Rooty.

He's constantly talking about the game, whether it's what's ahead or what has just happened. How the mood is around the group, who needs picking up and reassuring. He takes a lot on his shoulders, does Rooty, and he carries a lot with him as well. He takes it all personally. He's desperate to do well. He's a carer. He wants people to feel good. He's trying his best to improve everyone around him. He watched me for a whole net session in a drill where he stopped his practice, walked into the net next to me and started coaching me. He does that with everybody and even though he's not captain now, the fact he'll still be part of the team for a long time to come is a boost to all of us, especially those coming through.

Another person who is integral to it all is Mark Saxby. He's always good to chat to around the culture side of the group: keeping a lid on negative comments flying around behind closed doors and not letting people get away from the bigger picture of what we're doing – trying to be our best and win games for our country. Sax has been with England for donkey's years. I think he started out fluffing W.G. Grace's beard. He has become one of the most important people in our dressing room – someone who's in the dressing room but just enough removed that we can talk to him about anything, cricket or otherwise.

Sax is probably at his best when the cricket isn't going so well and we're getting it from all corners. He's good at telling us to ignore the noise, although cricket's the kind of game where you need to do that yourself to make it at this level.

Batters always talk about 'being in a bubble' but bowlers have that, too. We focus on the lengths we need to hit and the way we need to approach certain players.

But, as Mike Tyson famously didn't say, everyone has a plan until they get hit for six. Sometimes you lose sight of your plans just by who the other batter is. I've bowled plenty of balls at some of the best batters in the world and it doesn't really get easier.

Each one has his own distinct style and manner, meaning you're constantly cycling through different plans while also thinking, 'Oh god, not this bloke again.' More often than not, I still pinch myself, thinking, 'How good is it that I get to bowl at this bloke?'

With all of them, you have to really focus to ensure you're on the mark all the time because if you're off by the smallest amount, they smack you. And of course that means where you can try too hard, tense up, and be less effective. It's a precarious balancing act.

Someone like Virat Kohli makes you feel like you're in a fight. He's really in your face, even when he's not saying anything. He's got a confrontational style of batting. Each boundary feels like a punch to your gut and the onus is on you to shake it off.

At the other end of the spectrum is New Zealand's Kane Williamson. He's one of the nicest blokes you'll ever meet but he is utterly infuriating in every other way. It feels like he's batting with a barn door. He seems to hit every single ball out of the middle. But worst of all, every time he makes contact, he makes you think you're bowling much slower because it's so easy for him. There have been a few times when he's dabbed me into the ground that I've had to look at the speed on the screen to make sure I hadn't sent one down at 30 mph. Then he'll flick you off his legs or drive you down the ground.

Steve Smith's a bit like that. I've managed to get him out a few times, with both red and white ball, but you can always count on him to hurt us. He's so awkward to bowl at, not just because of his style but because pace never seems to affect him. You need to get everything right – the delivery, the field, the right people in the right positions, and so on. You basically spend weeks preparing for this one delivery to get him out. It's pretty draining.

The one batter who does give me nightmares is Rohit Sharma. His bat is wider, thicker and springier than everyone else's. He's got all the classical shots and, at the same time, can hit sixes with ease. It's annoying that he's so good to watch because sometimes I'll be going through the highlights and thinking, 'Ah, what a shot,' and then realize it's against me.

More often than not, these guys are always going to go all right. So you've got to almost maintain a bit of kidology. If they do drive you, give out an 'ooooh' to suggest they might have come close to edging it or hitting it straight to a fielder. Make it seem like they are playing your game, not theirs.

Similarly, it's about not giving too much away with your body language. Not getting too frustrated and losing your cool, especially with a teammate. Because if those players know you're fighting with each other, they grow stronger. If you're the one who hasn't gone well and someone in the field is annoyed, it can make you feel a bit self-conscious, too, especially if, say, the big screen shows them having a go at you behind your back. Isn't that right, Jos?

JOS BUTTLER: *Oh, yeah...*

MARK WOOD: *Let me set the scene. It was a limited-overs game in India and we had most of the fielders out on the leg side, so I had to get it straight or on leg stump to bowl to the field. Instead, I sent one down really full and wide of off stump. Rohit Sharma carted it over extra cover.*

Jos, who was captain, turned away in disgust. He didn't know this at the time, but a camera was on him and as I went to look at the big screen to see how I'd messed up, his face comes up. Now, I'm not the best lipreader, but I think it was something along the lines of 'rubbish ball, that'.

BUTTLER: *It might have been a 'rubbish ball', actually.*

WOOD: *It was, to be fair.*

BUTTLER: *I was looking at the big screen, too, which is why I kept facing the other way. I came up to you after the game and said, 'Mate, I've got to tell you this because it came up on the big screen, I don't know if you saw... but sorry!' Thankfully – or not – you had.*

★

The key to facing the best players is not putting these people on a pedestal. They aren't untouchable, they all go through bad trots. If you admire them then you're going to find it very hard to better them. Similarly, part of maintaining that sure mind yourself is to cut out all the external noise that can throw you off course.

I'm pretty good at that now, but there was certainly a period at the start of my England career when I would read everything and take it all too personally, especially on Twitter. I'd get loads of nice comments but only focus on the negatives. I wouldn't focus on the two thousand likes, I'd focus on the three or four negative comments. It wasn't like I believed them, but they still got me down.

I'd think, 'Why the hell are they saying that?' then obsess about what was said. But I feel as I've got older and more assured, I've been able to ignore the hurtful stuff. Deleting Twitter from my phone has helped.

As for abuse from the crowd, I'd like to say I've got that sussed but, to be honest, that still needs work.

I wouldn't say I get a lot of chat from the stands. Mainly it's stuff from Aussies. Highbrow stuff like 'Wood, you're an idiot', or asking me to sign their kid's bat, going over only to be greeted by a middle finger. Yeah, cheers, lads. Funnily enough, the times I've reacted most have been from English fans.

Durham were playing Gloucestershire in the quarter-final of the 2016 T20 Blast and there was a group of lads going at me. They were shouting about my injuries, and going on about how I wasn't any good. 'You're just a rubbish Steven Finn' got a few airings – I had to look twice to make sure they weren't my mates – and a lot of talk about how I'll never play for England again. 'One chance – and you cocked it up! One chance – and you cocked it up!'

I was getting more and more annoyed, and bowling faster and faster. When we won in the end – I ran out the non-striker in the nineteenth over of the chase while I was bowling – I ran over to them all. I was cupping my hand to my ear, offering them out for a fight (Can you imagine? Me, in a fight?) and shouting all sorts. Thankfully, the very sensible Keaton Jennings was there to grab me and pull me back to reality.

I also got abuse in my first Test match at Headingley – from England supporters as well! I thought the reception would be great. You know, it was the north, I'm from the north, and although I'm not from Yorkshire, they'll back me. The first time I went over to the Western Terrace some lad shouted, 'What are you doin' 'ere? Should be fookin' Plunkett!' Errr right, OK.

Also at that ground, I was bowling in a one-day game when they had the old stand at the bottom end. There was this one voice cutting through the crowd noise, just constantly telling me to 'hit the stooomps, lad'. 'Try hittin' fookin' stoooomps!' 'Come on, Wood, hit the stoomps!' Every ball for about three overs. By the end, I lost my rag, turned around and shouted, *Will you shut up!*' It turns out the bloke was in his eighties. I can still see his shocked little face now when I close my eyes. I'd just shouted at an eighty-year-old man. How bad a person am I?

I've come to accept that everyone has an opinion. I'm not saying I accept them all or that I think the way some of it is put across is good or deserves to be acknowledged. But deep down, I understand where it comes from. People love their cricket, especially Test cricket. And given how results have been in that format recently, I get why people are so emotional in their criticism of us and the team. I suppose the thing that irritates me is that I feel all this criticism. How can I not? Sometimes the criticism from the media and fans suggests that we don't.

Honestly, there is nothing worse than getting beaten in a series like the Ashes. It is relentless. It can feel like you've never got your whites off. You bowl, then you've got your batting kit on soon after, then the cycle continues again. Granted, we were getting a few more days off after because of how quickly we were getting beaten, but you feel the intensity of it so much more. There is no getting away from it. Though in the past we have done our best to avoid it.

It was the Lord's Test of the 2015 Ashes and we were already getting pumped after the first day. Australia were

337 for 1 and Chris Rogers (158 not out) and Steve Smith (129 not out) had big hundreds to their names. So, as you can imagine, we weren't exactly in a hurry to rock up for another day of being whooped in the field. That morning, I was in a car with Broad, Jimmy and Rooty, all of us deciding to get to the ground earlier, which is pretty common for bowlers. And, yes, I am including Rooty in that because he had to send a few overs down himself. Even Adam Lyth turned his arm over.

We were in the car, a bit sore, all feeling sorry for ourselves, when we got to a set of lights at Regent's Park. Suddenly, 'Hold Back the River' by James Bay – an absolute classic – comes on the car speakers. And just like that, the four James Bays in the car starting belting it out. We were getting so into it that Broady (the driver) decides to keep it going. We cue it up on an iPhone and listen to it over and over again, getting louder with each rendition, while doing laps of Regent's Park. I can only apologize now to fellow commuters on Park Road that morning. What must they have been thinking, looking over at a car full of lads pointing at each other going 'Lonely water, lonely water …'?

Now, Australia ended up making 566 for 8 in their first innings and went on to win by 406 runs. But that car ride to me summed up how important it is to share the tough moments with each other. You can spend a lot of time in life struggling on your own, thinking no one else knows what you're going through. I certainly had moments like that in my career, whether it was injury or just doubting my ability, where I closed myself off and ended up feeling worse about it. But one thing I've learned is how common that doubt is among teammates and opponents.

I'll never forget a chat we had during the 2019 World Cup. We'd lost three games and had three left to play in the group stage, with the knockouts looking a bit dicey at this point, with India up next at Edgbaston. I say it was a chat, but you could probably upgrade it to 'meeting'. The session was run by David Young, the England sports psychologist, who is now head of psychology at Manchester City. He split us up into different groups and got us to talk about how it would make us feel if we went out. A simple question, really, with a pretty simple answer: awful, rubbish, miserable. Any of the above. But the fact we were discussing this was important because what we realized was we all had these fears. This was just the first time we were putting them out in the open.

The next part was us talking about our individual fears. I told the group that I've been nervous in the field ever since I had dropped Chris Gayle down at fine leg in our fourth match, which we won comfortably by eight wickets. I said, 'If we reached the final, I'd be worried about making a similar mistake. What happens if I drop the catch and they win the game?' That had been eating me up inside for weeks.

Just putting it out there was a massive relief, as was hearing that others had similar fears. The one that shocked me the most was Stokesy, who said he was nervous before games and felt worried he'd just let us down. All of us were in shock. We'd never heard him say something like that. He was in form and he never backs down, always takes the positive option. And here he was... just like us. Eoin Morgan said similar, and Jason Roy, too. Confident lads who didn't seem to have any self-doubt. Among all that, it got us back focusing how we'd been as a group, how we wanted to play, how we wanted to be perceived, how we wanted to be with each other. It was the perfect session.

★

One of the conversations that gets harder the more you play is when a coach or captain tells you you're not playing. No matter if it's for tactical reasons, it's always a bump to your ego. When you're in the squad you know you've been picked for a reason, so you always come with a sense you're good enough to make the starting XI. Then when you're told you're not part of it, there's a mixture of disappointment, anger and frustration that you've got to wait your turn. It's particularly annoying when it's for a Test match because that's a lot of time on the sidelines doing nowt. Well, not quite doing nowt. Because the most irritating thing about not playing is having to be one of the twelfth men...

MARK WOOD'S GUIDE TO TWELFTH-MANNING

I think the best way to describe being a twelfth man is that you're a butler without the nice suit. You have to wait on everyone who is playing, helping them out with whatever they need and also potentially coming on as a substitute if anyone gets injured.

The last time I had a shift as twelfth man was during the day–night Test at Adelaide during the 2021/22 Ashes.

Normally what you do is you split the duty into three shifts: morning, afternoon and evening. And because that was a day–night Test, the final shift was late. However, the previous Test, Anderson and Broad weren't playing. So, as the establishment, they decided upon a new system, which basically meant specific people had designated roles. One of those was Craig Overton, who in this new order was always doing the final shift of the day, which went on until 11 p.m. local time.

It was not just because he was the most junior, but because of his superhuman ability to sleep at any time of day. He's the best sleeper I've ever seen, even trumps Jofra.

When Craig Overton lies down, he falls asleep. It doesn't matter where he is or how loud it is. He can lie on a cricket bag. He can lie on a cricket *bat*.

I remember at Sydney, there were three or four bowlers getting treatment in this area at the back of the dressing room. It was loud, there were ice machines going, showers on, chat in the room with the TV on. Right in the middle was Craig, fast asleep on the floor.

So, as I was saying: you've got morning, afternoon and night shifts. Normally you might do two out of the three sessions or just one because we had a bigger squad. But The Hierarchy had decided that, no, we – those not playing – will do the shifts when we are batting, which is obviously easier because there's no fielding involved, and that's always on the cards when we're bowling. Given the way we were batting in that series, it worked quite well for them.

When we got to Adelaide, because I was a bowler, I got to take over Broad and Anderson's batting shifts because they were both playing. Plus, the management wouldn't want me to field because I'm not the best fielder.

Initially, we are fielding so I have a lot of time on my hands: I'm getting some bowling done, getting the gym done, everything like that. What I fail to realize is that when we start batting, the shift clocks on. There is no handover, no covering for you if you're not back in time. It's every twelfth man for himself.

You're aways in your whites and you get a specialized bib that smells fresh at the start of the game and by the end smells like it's been pulled out of a rotten dumpster. It has that vinegary bitter smell – awful.

You've got a checklist of things to keep on top of: towels,

a batter's spare gloves, spare bats, that kind of thing. You have to know your player.

Dawid Malan, for example, will want glove changes every four overs. Others have a specific order they want gloves in and number them. Jos Buttler names his after footballers: Shearer, Pelé, De Bruyne. Dom Sibley had about fifty headbands because he sweats that much.

Root often wants bats and before play he'll talk you through his spares. If he calls for one when the first choice breaks or is cracked, it'll be one bat. But if he's in a certain stage of his innings, it'll be a different one.

I'm not quite that particular, though I am superstitious when it comes to boots. If I bowl well, I'll keep them. Otherwise, like when I did OK in the Champions Trophy but took only five wickets, I decided to toss them. Usually, I get them in bulk from my sponsor and label them. It started with numbers, then different coloured dots.

I've moved on to more creative labelling. I went through a phase of drawing Xs, triangles, squares and circles in homage to the PlayStation controls. The load I got last winter were named after *Mario Kart* characters, starting with Yoshi, my favourite. I've got my Wahluigi ones for when I'm feeling especially mischievous. When I want to bring my inner demon out I'll bring out my Bowsers. If I want to bowl quick I'll do the Cooper Troopers.

Then there's the drinks: are they topped up? Are they cool enough? Some people like water, some like juice. Some people like them ice cold, some like them room temperature. Do you have the spray for Stokesy's hands that stop them from sweating? There's a lot to keep across.

Jack Leach, Craig Overton and I ended up doing a few shifts together. We got that bored one day we decided to play 'The Humming Game'. We quickly moved on to solving life problems. Leachy and I then started settling old, fake arguments. Basically looking back on times when, say, we were dropped and just accepted it but now looking at it and thinking, what we should have said but in overly dramatic ways: 'You're dropped for the next Test.' 'Yeah, well I'm going to drop you.' That kind of stuff.

There was some actual waitering to be done as well. If the batters were sat in the changing room and didn't want to go to the dining room to get their lunch, we had to go and get it for them. To be fair, bowlers are more likely to do that because they are knackered so they want food brought to them.

I'd like to say I'm not as demanding when the bib is on the other, well, person. But I'm sure others will disagree. It's just a shame they weren't available to talk in this book, as it's my book...

★

I still remember, aged twenty-one, sat in the car park of Newcastle College, wondering if I'd ever make it as a cricketer. At the time, I was with Durham but I felt they had been stringing me along with academy contracts that were only for a summer. I was in that particular car park because I'd joined the college to further my education. My dad instilled in us to get an education as a backup. I'd had an offer of a scholarship to Newcastle University where they wanted me to play cricket. But I decided to go to college to do it on my own terms.

Sat there, I knew my heart wasn't in that because I was desperate to make cricket work. But I felt like I was banging my head against a brick wall. I was on the phone to the academy director John Windows – he'd actually called to congratulate us on getting another academy contract. I remember thinking, 'Academy? They haven't even given me a development contract!' I'd made my first-team debut and was posting good numbers in the second XI and academy. And I was only injured just the once! I thought I deserved more.

I let him know what I thought, but I tried not to be too moany. I've never liked complaining about not getting stuff. It feels entitled and that's not how I want to be. It fired us up to go and show them they had made a mistake. I didn't like complaining, but I felt I had every right to feel annoyed. Eventually, at twenty-three, I got a proper contract and it felt like a big deal. It felt like I was a part of something. You felt like it was the first step. Not that you made it, but there was a bit of relief that I was in the club and that they rated me. Before that point, I wondered if they did.

I realized that it doesn't matter what level you play, or who you play for – everyone worries. It's just that not everyone talks about it. And I suppose that's fine. Some people don't like to show weakness or be that open with other people. I know I can be a bit like that sometimes, which makes me a bit of a hypocrite because when I see someone down, I just want them to tell me what's wrong. I know I might not be able to fix it straight away, but I hate seeing people upset.

The worst thing when a series is going badly is the wondering why. Why is this happening? You're training hard in the nets. Granted, it's a bit different with Covid, there are more pressures away from the cricket. You turn up to a game, as we did in Adelaide and Sydney, and there's a Covid situation. That's not normal, is it? You can't do things, you're restricted, you have to do PCR tests every day. But you look around at good players and can't explain why we're not getting it right. All the while you know if it keeps going that way, people are going to lose their places and their jobs.

I think the toughest was on the 2021/22 Australia tour during the Adelaide Test. I wasn't playing, but I was sat next to Jos in the changing room. He was having a rough Test and in a real bad way. He'd had a few costly drops, including Marnus Labuschagne before he went on to get a hundred. At the end of one of the days, I noticed he got changed really quickly and was just sat in his seat while everyone was bustling around the changing room. A lot of people think he's quiet, but he was even quieter than normal. He wasn't saying anything, no input in chats, which is very unlike him. He was a bit fidgety, too: picking at his eyebrow, touching his nose, stroking his beard. As I mentioned before, you can tell when Jos is upset or angry because the whites of his eyes go really red.

I spoke to James Foster, who said he was pretty rotten because of the error. Wicketkeeping is bit like goalkeeping: you can make a million good saves but everybody notices the mistakes. I decided to chat to Jos to try and take his mind off what had happened. I got the team manager to get us one of the team cars so we could get back to the hotel quickly and not have to wait for the bus. I gave him a nudge and said, 'Come on now, let's get in the car.' I wanted to get him away from a cricket ground as quickly as possible.

When we got back to the hotel, Fozzie and I tried to get him to come for a drink but he kept saying no. We left it in his court, telling him we'd be at the top floor for one drink and that he should join us. Eventually, Jos came up and it was great to just know we were making a small difference and that he wasn't stewing on it alone.

JOS BUTTLER: *I needed that. You are someone who has a good read on people. You can tell where they are at, when they've had a tough day. I feel like you've got great empathy so you can pick up on that and are never shy of saying something.*

MARK WOOD: *Sometimes you don't know whether you should or not. I've definitely tried to do stuff like that and made things worse.*

BUTTLER: *I think in times when someone has had a hard day, you know they are feeling bad and sometimes you think it's best to leave them. But Woody, I'd say you are always someone who'd want to show his support. Even if it's just a pat on the back or to say if you need to chat, I'm here. You'll always make the effort. At the time you might think it's the last thing someone needs, but actually to force that situation is brilliant, every time. It's something you always do really well. Just another huge asset for everyone. Woody has that jokey personality but he gets a great read on the group and other individuals.*

WOOD: *What am I like when I'm in that mood?*

BUTTLER: *I'd say you go quite insular. You can tell you're either angry or disappointed. You'll just hold it for a bit and go really quiet. Someone's then got to break the ice with you and you're like a jack-in-the-box, springing back up and being the joker again. You're not as bad as J-Roy, but you're on the same rollercoaster.*

WOOD: *As if I'm on the same scale as J-Roy! Now he's someone you can't joke with straight away. Just avoid, avoid, avoid. He's a kit thrower, a massive shouter – always at himself, to be fair. 'What are you doing?!' 'You* *idiot!' That kind of stuff. Even when he's done well, he'll be furious that he's got out but then get back up and bounce off the walls. Rollercoaster Roy.*

There was a funny moment against New Zealand for a warm-up game in the UAE ahead of the 2021 T20 World Cup. He walked at the first ball and got bowled around his legs. We expected a blow-up. Instead, he just goes 'Oh, brilliant,' turns around and walks off. As he got back to the changing room he put one foot in the door and goes, 'I guess I should go to the nets, then,' and walked all the way through, without taking any of his kit off, and straight to the nets out the back.

I think Jos is the one whose disappointment hurts me the most. He's done so much for our team and brought the rest of us, and the fans, so much joy. Not that Jos would read my book, but if he does, I hope he'll realize how much everybody thinks of him. I think so highly of him, not just as a cricketer but as a bloke as well.

He had to leave after the Fourth Test because he broke a finger stopping a ball off me that kept a bit low. He was having two injections every session to numb the pain and get him through the game and ended up going out there and batting on the final day to help us save the Test. Those 38 balls chewed up with a busted hand were vital in the end.

I probably shouldn't say that I was jealous of him getting home a game early. He'd have wanted to stay on and, to be honest, the final Test in Hobart was the best of the lot for me. But the toll of being away for that long was wearing me down. Christmas was a heartbreaker, watching Harry tearing through wrapping paper over FaceTime. I reckon at the age of two, kids start to understand what Christmas is and he was mad about it. Sarah propped the phone up on the side for a good view, but he was moving around so much that I reckon I got about 10 per cent of him opening his presents.

Worst of all was he started saying to Sarah 'love Daddy', 'Daddy come home' and 'Daddy and Harry go to John lock-up', which is basically a digger site. I think it was the first time he was able to say he misses me, which was gut-wrenching to hear. But having the bigger picture of the Ashes helped. I knew I was away from Sarah and Harry for a reason, and I knew they knew that too. Well, Sarah certainly did. Harry, well, I'll just have to explain that to him when he's older. Probably when we're rewatching highlights of my spell at Hobart.

Still, the team was able to crack on. Not very well, mind, but there were moments to cling on to like lifeboats. Jonny Bairstow's hundred at Sydney was definitely one. There have been a few times players have got a hundred and I've found it emotional. Jonny's one was in that bracket. I was so pleased for him because I know what he's been through. The stuff we'd talked about: the times he felt Test cricket wouldn't happen for him again, the frustrations of being in and out of the team, up and down the order. I was teary-eyed and a bit overwhelmed.

JONNY BAIRSTOW: *Yeah, that was so sweet. I didn't play in that Hobart game but I couldn't have been more happy for you. It was a role reversal for what you felt in Sydney: I was exactly the same. We've played against each other since 11 years old and then played with each other for a long period of time now with England. So we've built up a relationship through that. Naturally there's a common ground there with being from the north, but as a bloke and a character we get on well together. Being able to have those honest conversations, especially when you're on tour, is important. You're able to offload stuff onto me, and vice versa.*

Alastair Cook's double hundred at Melbourne in the 2017 Ashes Test was pretty emotional. He was in tears when he came into the dressing room after it. I think he was under so much pressure. I don't know if maybe he thought he'd lost it or was lacking belief in himself. But that was amazing.

Similarly, I had a lump in my throat for Stokesy's hundred at Lord's against New Zealand in 2015. There had been doubts about him, such as not going to the fifty-over World Cup earlier that year. Obviously, I know him well and knew what he was going through, and he just went out there and spanked it. He ended up getting the fastest hundred at Lord's by an Englishman.

Then there was Jos's century against Australia in an ODI at Sydney, 2018. That was a proper 'getting caught up in the moment' one, because we were reeling on 172 for 5, then Jos got us to 302 from our fifty overs, getting to 100 off the last ball. We ended up winning by 16 runs and taking the series. Morgan against Afghanistan in the 2019 World Cup was another heartstrings-plucker because the day before he literally couldn't walk. He had an epidural in his back then went out and chinned 17 sixes to score 148.

I suppose when it's all said and done, even losing an Ashes series is a privilege in a way. Not ideal, sure. Rubbish? Yes. But I played my first Test series in Australia, off the back of my first T20 World Cup – two things I can say I've done without needing to go too heavy on the details. Plus I'll have another crack at both soon enough.

Even in those tough periods, it's still the best job in the world. Something I'd never thought I'd do. And when I arrived home and walked through the front door after three months apart, Harry did have that big smile on his face. Though I know it was really for Lucas the Spider.

8

HOW TO BE TRUE
TO YOURSELF

never felt the need to change how I speak just because I play for England. I don't really know why you would, or even why my mates think it's good that I don't.

DANIEL GRANT: *You see a few of the lads in interviews and you can tell they're trying to 'talk properly'. Or, as we and Woody would say, 'talk proper'. But he sounds exactly the same everywhere. I do like that he doesn't hide it.*

GLEN TAYLOR: *I listen to his interviews and he'll just say 'naw' and 'nar'. He'll never come away from that.*

JONNY STOREY: *It's good that he doesn't change his accent just to fit in.*

GRANT: *I remember the ECB released a video where he was teaching phrases to Sam Billings. They had to put subtitles on Woody!*

It doesn't bother us when people take the mickey out of my accent, I'm fine with that. Stokesy's wife, Clare, often tells me off for influencing him, because when we chat his accent goes up a few notches and she canny stand it: 'I hate it when Ben hangs out with you because he starts saying "fuirbal" instead of "football".'

Having a strong accent like mine can maybe sound more common. But I like that. I'm not posh, and I don't want to be posh. As a kid, we didn't like posh people all that much. They get everything given to them, think they're it and turn their noses up at people like us. When we used to play cricket against the posh teams Jesmond or South Northumberland, we hated it. They thought they were better than you and that was extra motivation. They had money, had this high opinion of themselves and it was up to us to bring them back down to earth.

I love my accent and that's reinforced by me mam. Me mam's accent is really strong because of how and where she grew up. She's from Newbiggin-by-the-Sea, by the coast next to Ashington. She had a tough upbringing as one of seven kids and they didn't have very much money. It wasn't easy for them. People used to say to her, oh you're speaking Norwegian, Swahili or like a fishmonger's wife. And Mam's reaction would always be the same: 'So what?' I can hear her voice and see her face as she says it. Why does it matter? Why does it bother you?

That's the attitude I have. I'm going to be who I'm going to be. Have a go. Have fun. This is who you are – embrace it. Who cares how you talk? Just be a good person. So what? Who cares? Be proud of who you are.

ANGELA WOOD: *It still annoys me that when we go abroad people say we're Geordies. No, we're not Geordies – we're Northumbrian!*

MARK WOOD: *The Ashington accent is more Pitmatic: a dialect from the pits that's a bit sharper. Whereas Geordie has a bit of a drawl. For example, a Geoooordie 'would tooork very much laike this'. They'd say 'nooooor' (no), 'bist in the wuuuurld'. Whereas if you're from Ashington you'd say 'neeeer', 'best in the woruld'. If you gan to Sunderland it's even worse. We'd say 'curry', they'd say 'kerry'. I actually got started on once in Sunderland. I was meeting the Durham lads in a bar after an academy game. I went to the bar, said hullo and asked for a lemonade. This lad at the bar heard me and went, 'Where are you-er fram?' 'I'm from Ashington.' 'Oh, so you're a Geordie?' 'No, I'm not a Geordie, mate...' Then out of nowhere, one of my teammates from Sunderland comes in and goes, 'Woah woah woah – don't worry, he's with us.' Geez, I was there for one minute!*

★

People always say England players have a lot of media training. That's not actually true. The only time I had anything like that was when I was with the England Lions and we had one session on how to prepare for interviews. Because we were close to breaking into the full England team, there'd be more requests to speak to us. I remember speaking to someone at the ECB about how to approach media engagements and at the end of it they said I'd be absolutely fine just being myself.

If you don't bring your personality into it, you'd be boring. I know it's cricket and it's all very serious, especially Test cricket, but you've got to bring your own genuine side into it. Of course, it depends on your own parameters, whatever you do in life and whatever the situation, but you need to be honest to yourself and whatever it is you're talking about. If something was rubbish, say it was rubbish.

When things are rubbish for England and we've had a bad day, I know I get put up more than most and I'm fine with that. The team media manager Danny Reuben is one of the most genuine people you can meet and I've got great respect for him. He's basically the middleman between us and the press and it says a lot that he's popular on both sides because it's a tricky balance to strike. He advises us on how to be in interviews and looks after us in that regard. His job is a little harder when we lose because obviously players don't want to do any media. Sometimes he'll convince us to do stuff, other times, if things are really bad, he's great at shielding us from it. The way he and other staff members work for us, it really reinforces that we are all a team, that we are all in this together, even if only eleven of us go out onto the field. Everyone is trying to do their best for the England team.

Of course, it's not easy and sometimes I think the tactic of putting me up after we've been pumped is a bit 'roll out the jester!' But it doesn't bother us at all. I like being honest and having a bit of character about it as well. Even when it's tough, I don't feel I have to be anybody that I'm not. If I'm just who I am in the dressing room, and everywhere else, that's hopefully good enough.

When people say you're a joker or you're this or that, I wouldn't say I purposely go out and do that or try to lift people's spirits. Sometimes the feedback is positive: that I had good energy, humorous while getting the right message across. Sometimes I might get off track and Dad will message saying, 'Ooof, you shouldn't have said that, the press will be all over you.'

But I don't make a conscious effort to be what you see in the media. Because when I do try too hard, it doesn't go down too well. Like when I did a guest appearance on the Aggers and Tuffers tour and made a crude joke. That didn't really land. Probably not my target audience, to be honest, but you've got to have material for everybody. Even if they aren't in the crowd ...

That's basically how I used to approach social media when I was more active on it. Just sitting around, firing off my random thoughts into the ether. I never thought anyone would be interested in them, mind. It was a good way of killing time and chatting to fans. Now, though, I think it's rare for athletes to have direct access to their social media. But for a while I enjoyed it as an outlet for my stupidity.

★

I'll admit to trying too hard to be funny at school. I think almost every report card had: 'Mark is a very talented student but continues to disrupt the class.' Humour was kind of my thing because I didn't have a commanding presence at school, unlike my mate Jonny Storey who was a brick wall and a fighter. I almost saw it as my responsibility to make everybody have a good time and there were moments I tried too hard.

I remember in French class we were doing this exercise where we had to cut bits out of magazines and stick them on a bit of card. There was a girl sat in front of me and she kept leaning back so her ponytail would come onto my desk. I was getting more and more annoyed about it. She leant back one last time and, as a reaction, I cut a bit of her hair off. She jumped up screaming and was in floods of tears. Immediately I thought, 'Mark, why the hell have you done that?'

I got sent to our head of year and was waiting to be suspended. As it happens, he was also our school football coach and I was the football captain. The meeting reflected as much.

'Been cutting girls' hair off I hear, Woody?'

'Yes, sir. Sorry, I don't know what I was thinking.'

'You're not going to do that again now, are you?'

'No, sir.'

'OK, I'll see you for training tonight. Champagne football, remember.'

I went back and apologized to the girl but I still feel awful about it to this day. Sadly, it wasn't the worst thing I did.

There was a teacher we had who must have been in her early twenties. She used to sit at her desk at the front of the class, doing these magazine questionnaires on things like her horoscope, that kind of stuff. One time when she had her back turned, I ran and nicked one of her magazines and took it to the back of the class where the lad sat next to me, Nelson, stood up and read out what she had been writing. It turns out this particular questionnaire was on her love life and what kind of man and relationship she'd be suited to. She ended up bursting into tears and running out of the classroom. Thinking about it now, what an arsey thing for us to have done. I felt dreadful. Why have I showed off like that?

I'd like to think I've grown out of that now, especially having a joke at someone's expense. I suppose that's just maturing, really. Trying to make yourself feel better by making someone else feel worse is never healthy or productive. Unless they're 22 yards away from you and holding a bat.

JOE ROOT: *You definitely don't put other people down for a laugh, but you haven't grown up either! Before the 2015 Ashes, we had a trip to Desert Springs in Spain as a training camp. On a day off, we all cycled down to this beach. When we got there, we saw a sign that it was a nudist beach, which none of us realized when we set off. As we're all settling in, suddenly Woody comes flying by on his bike with nothing but his trainers on. He was the only naked one on the beach.*

MARK WOOD: *Even I can't believe that. It was my first summer as an England cricketer. What was I doing? As a senior player now, if someone came into the dressing room and did that, I'd tell them to pack it in.*

PHIL SCOTT: *Well... you still do it now. There are times I've come into the gym and you'll be doing naked squats. You do it so often now that some of the players are used to it when they shouldn't be!*

★

The industrial history of Ashington was drummed into us as a kid. Not just on school trips to the local museums and stuff like that. It was all around you.

You only need to drive two minutes up the road from my parents' house to see the two shaft lifts popping out over the top of everything. All the rows of terrace houses that seem to go on for ever tucked arm-in-arm together. The quarry that remains dormant.

There was a time when Ashington was known as the largest coal-mining village in the world. The colliery here was opened in 1867 and went on to help us grow from a village to a town that punched well above its weight. The pits in the town were among 200 across Northumberland and Durham, and, at the end of the Second World War, there were 148,000 men employed in the region's mines. The economy was booming and the togetherness of the region thrived as a result. Pitmen looked after each other, families did the same and there was a real sense of community throughout. A lot of the stuff that remains a key part of what it is to be from Ashington today.

Both my grandads were pitmen. My dad's grandad was a pitman, and his dad too. Mam's brother was also a pitman. My dad's dad, Dennis Wood, who is still around, actually had to retire when he broke his ankle severely in a mining accident. I always tell him I got my dicky ankle from him.

I was the only grandchild on Dennis's side so I spent more time with him, whereas my mam's dad has like twenty, so he was spoilt for choice.

When the Ashington pit closed in 1986, our family was one of many devastated. The whole community suddenly had the rug pulled out from under us. The heavy industries left soon after, and the sense of camaraderie isn't what it was. There remains a lot of hatred about what happened then. As you can imagine, the Conservative party aren't popular up here and I've always been a staunch Labour supporter. When I was thirteen years old, I leafleted for our Labour candidate, Ian Lavery. If you ever visit Ashington, I'd advise you not to bring Margaret Thatcher up. We had the bunting out at Ashington when Thatcher died.

I'm proud of my mining heritage because of what they went through to build this town up and guide us, and I'm proud of being working class. I suppose folk will say because I play for England and get paid well that I'm not working class any more. But it's part of who I am. Those experiences are the reason I am who I am today, and I'm not going to lose that. Just little things like making sure you're grounded, not taking yourself too seriously and even that black sense of humour. All of those elements come from growing up around here.

Cricket in England is obviously a posh sport, but I don't consider myself a poster boy for working-class kids. The way I see it, I'm a normal lad who has been lucky to play for England. I don't necessarily feel like a representative of where I am from in that I don't think people should look at me as if all people from my part of the world are like me. But I feel proud to represent England, Durham, Northumberland and Ashington.

DANIEL GRANT: *I talk to a bunch of people and end up talking about cricket and everyone will mention Woody's name before I mention it. And they always mention Ashington. It's weird. They don't see him as a Durham cricketer, they see him as an Ashington cricketer. Which is probably no mistake on Woody's part.*

JONNY STOREY: *Yeah, nobody ever says Durham. Nobody says, say, 'Rory Burns...' and then where he lives. Him and Harmy have helped put Ashington on the map.*

SCOTT DUNN: *The same goes for his teammates and their families. Whenever they see us at a game supporting Woody, they always refer to us as 'The Ashington Boys'.*

I do think it's important to state where I'm from, or state how much I enjoy living here, and I'll always praise this place. I haven't felt the need to push it, but if it ever comes up, I'd never back down from sticking up for it. My mentality is my place is as good as yours. Maybe even better.

I think that's something I realized watching Stephen Harmison. I've always had a connection with Harmy because he was a close family friend. And having someone in your circle who did what he did made us believe I could, too.

He was best mates with my uncle Neil, who was basically my hero growing up. Uncle Neil was a hell of a player, one of the best batters in the region. I used to give him throw-downs before he was waiting to bat so I perfected half-volleys.

One year the club secretary, Dale Ross, decided it would be funny to apply for a job at McDonald's on my behalf. Under 'hobbies' he put 'Playing cricket with my uncle Neil'. Any other interests? 'Spending time with my uncle Neil'. The whole thing was a love letter to my uncle Neil. Obviously Ronald McDonald holds my uncle Neil in high regard too because they gave me a job interview.

Harmy was very much one of our own, and the town was so proud to have someone like him playing for England. This demon fast bowler who was terrorizing the best batters to have played the game. That first day of the 2005 Ashes when he bounced Ponting and drew blood basically set the tone for the rest of that famous series. That 7 for 12 he got in the West Indies, too – mental figures.

When I first got picked for England, Harmy congratulated us and talked about how much of what I knew was going to change. He encouraged us to be myself and continue to be who I was. To hear it from someone who had played 63 Tests for his country and had a couple of Ashes winner's medals reinforced that sense I didn't need to compromise myself to fit in.

STEPHEN HARMISON: *Even with the family connection, there was always a duty to help Mark. When I played, like*

Mark, I felt a responsibility that I wanted to be the best I possibly could to make my town proud. I always felt every time I came back, it was to make sure the people of Ashington were proud of you, whether it was a game for England or Durham. Because – and Mark gets this as well – because you are the community. You're representing the people who helped make who you are. Not just your parents but the people from the surrounding area who influenced you.

I probably broke the mould for our generations as a lot of the people around hadn't seen the Charltons or Jackie Milburn. It was a long time since that. Then all of a sudden, when you walk down the street, people look at you as someone who fulfilled the dream from this area to play professional sport and play for England. Mark is that now. If you've got somebody to look up to, to aspire to, especially like Mark who is a good role model, there will be a conveyor belt of people coming through the community.

Whenever Harmy used to come back to Ashington after an England series or tour, he'd always bring back loads of kit from the players. Unfortunately, given he was six-foot-five and wore size-twelve boots, all his stuff would be memorabilia. But he'd always have kit from other players in the dressing room, whether they were bats, gloves, pads or playing shirts. That was something I make sure to do every time I'm away with England.

We get so well looked after with kit. Every game pretty much we get brand-new whites, and sponsors always send us more bats and boots than we'll ever need. So, more often than not, at the end of a series, players just throw away their stuff. They know now that I'm always lurking for bits they don't need any more. It's not all one way. Rooty and I are both sponsored by New Balance and one time he picked up one of my bats, scored a hundred in a game and decided to keep it. See – even someone like Rooty is after my stash.

SEAN 'SHEEP' MCCAFFERTY: *When he comes back from a tour, it's the best thing in the world because it's like Christmas for cricket kit. I don't know how he flies it all back, there's so much stuff. I can't remember the last time I paid for any cricket kit. But he can't wait to bring stuff back for everybody. The opposition often take the mickey out of us because we're all New Balance-d up and it is quite awkward when numbers one to five all walk out in England helmets.*

JONNY STOREY: *I remember I was batting against South Northumberland once, head to toe in Woody's gear, and the slip cordon were taking the mickey out of us. 'Awwww cute, did your mate Woody get this for you? Is he your best mate? Are you wearing his boxers as well?' I turned around and said, 'Lads, this is what happens when your club produces England players – you get stuff.' They went quiet after that.*

It might seem a small thing, but I see it as a way of paying things forward. As much as you can inspire people around you with what you do, doing a bit extra – even something small like giving someone kit – makes such a big difference. Because part of the responsibility in that situation is to help people out. There is probably a lot in life people take for granted just because they get it for free, and kit can be one of those things for a cricketer.

Things like signed shirts that get auctioned can raise a lot of money for your club. When you see the faces of young kids light up when you give them a pair of Jos's keeping gloves, Jonny's pads, one of Rooty's old bats or a ball signed by Jimmy, you can tell it means the world to them. Even older players who work nine-to-five or night shifts and then spend that money watching us play cricket – it's a way to make them all feel connected to the England team. We're representing them, after all.

STEPHEN HARMISON: *I'd always say at the end of a tour or series: 'Put it in a bag and I'll find it a good home.' It'll mean something to them. That's the area we're from. It's not tight-fisted, it's just knowing the value of stuff beyond money.*

MARK WOOD: *I see people with my tops on and that. I'm happy to give back to my club and help them with kit because it's special to them. I don't get a kick out of it, but I'm pleased to make them happy that they can wear* *it. Even in a funny way, that they don't have to pay for stuff because cricket kit is expensive! I know what it was growing up and if you got something off an England player you were like, 'Wow, this is amazing!'*

HARMISON: *You go around Ashington today and you see Woody's legacy. All the kids are trying to be him. Even my son Charlie adores Woody. Half of his kitbag is from Woody: he's got a refurbished bat from the dressing room and a pair of Woody's pads. He's only thirteen so he'll fly through the size eight-and-a-half boots Woody gave to him.*

WOOD: *Look, for one thing they are size nines, which is average in the UK, I think. And at least he'll get use out of them, more than us with the wall brackets you used to give us.*

★

I think everybody needs to have a solid grounding. You always need something to go back to. That might be a group of people or a place, sometimes it can just be a thought or a sense you have ingrained in you. As you go through life, things pull you different ways, and it's important to know how to reset yourself. To have something that brings you back to your true self. And when you're back there, you can take stock. Look around at the things in your life and try and work out how to stop them getting you off-course in the future.

For me, my sense of self and what's right came from my parents. They allowed us to find my own way, guiding me throughout but always letting me go off and become my own person. They'd only ever have a go at us if they felt I was losing sight of myself, like when Mam had a go at us for buying that honking Armani shirt. Even then, they let me make my own mistakes and never judged us too harshly. They were always there at my lowest moments. I know you might be thinking, 'Well, that's what parents do.' But you can sometimes forget about that unconditional love when you're in your own head. Being able to live this life, being able to play cricket and enjoy it with them, that's my way of trying to pay that back.

DEREK WOOD: *All we tried to do is instil some reasonable values and say: these are the things, the beliefs and values you should have. How you should be true to yourself and all the rest of it.*

ANGELA WOOD: *Whenever I'm out with my friends, they'll always bring Mark up. 'Do you know who her son is?' I don't like that too much, but whoever they say it to always talks about how much they love Woody.*

DEREK: *There have been a few times where I've been bursting with pride at the cricket, when you see what he means to people. On his debut at Lord's, there was a fantastic atmo-*

sphere at the ground and as I was walking in I suddenly realized: 'These people are coming to watch our son play.' At the end of that summer, when they were walking around The Oval and he had the urn, I was emotional. I'm usually quite calm when I watch him, though don't get me wrong, I get angry when he throws his wicket away like a muppet. But that day I had a lump in my throat.

ANGELA: *When he was a toddler, my sister used to babysit him during the day. She used to take him to the paper shop around the corner so he could buy sweets. One time I went in there with him, and the woman behind the counter asked who I was. I told her I'm his mam and she went on about how he was the only one who comes in and says please and thank you.*

DEREK: *I think the readers were probably looking for a moment in cricket that made you proud...*

ANGELA: *I know, but that's just the first thing that came to mind! I know it's silly, but for someone to say that about your toddler son, for him to even know that stuff is important. I felt we'd done all right with him then.*

DEREK: *Quite often, when people say to us, 'You must be very proud of him,' they are talking about him as a cricketer. My stock reply is I'm proud of him as a lad, I'm proud of him as a person, I'm proud of the man he is becoming.*

MARK WOOD: *That's class, isn't it? I don't know if every-one's the same as me, but often you'd seek your parents' approval and you'd want them to be proud of you. I'm glad that they don't see us as Mark the cricketer but as Mark their son. Making them proud as a person is prob-ably a million times better than them saying they are proud of us just because I play cricket for England.*

★

One thing playing sport professionally has done for me is establish a sense of belonging beyond Ashington, beyond my friends and family. You're judged harshly by what we do and, with cricket being such a numbers game, there are always markers you are constantly wanting to reach. I want to win more series. I want to win an Ashes in Australia if I'm still able to be at my best, given I'll be thirty-four in 2024/25. I'd love us to win a Twenty20 World Cup and defend our fifty-over one in 2023. And now that I'm getting a good run in Test cricket, I'd love to get my bowling average below 30.

I'm stating the obvious here, but I know those are just statistics. They are just things that help you feel like you've made more of yourself, but they don't sum up what I've done or define us as a person. And at the same time, what I've always accomplished gives me a belief that I belong to a world I didn't think I'd ever be a part of. Think of all the great England cricketers who haven't won a World Cup or an Ashes. All the greats who have had to give up the game they love because it was taken from them.

It's why I'm so keen to share as much of it as possible with those around me. I joke about how the lads had a great time celebrating my success over the years, but they are as much their experiences as mine. The people I love show me more of what I am than a Test bowling average (it's 31.91, by the way) or how many wickets I've taken in whites. (I'm 18 off 100 wickets, if you're counting, which I definitely am not. Oh, 69 in ODIs too, seeing as you're asking, at the time of writing this.)

That day at The Oval in 2015, after my mates had gatecrashed the celebrations in the changing rooms, I took them along to the afterparty at this fancy hotel. There was a moment when all of us were stood in a circle on this balcony: me, Jonny Storey, Glen Taylor and another mate, Josh Robinson, who is a mate from school since I was a kid and is the current second team captain at Ashington. Jonny had my medal around his neck, Glen was wearing my cap and I think Josh still had a bottle of champagne on the go. Just four lads from a local town, who'd known each other their whole lives, looking out onto London from on high, wondering how we got here.

JONNY STOREY: *I was quite emotional and couldn't hold it in. 'How have we got to this point? People like us shouldn't be here.' At that point, Woody pulled me in tight and got us all to come a bit closer. He looked us all in the eye and... well, I wonder if he remembers what he said?*

MARK WOOD: *I do. Because I meant it. I said people like us should be here. We deserve to be here, man. That's why we're here. They are the moments you always remember. We'll still talk about that balcony in twenty years. When you think of some of the daft stuff we've done together, that was one of the cool things.*

STOREY: *And then we burst into tears.*

9

Q & A

While researching self-help books – a long old slog, you'll surely believe – I realized quite a few of them have a section of questions for you to answer. The kind where your responses say a lot about the kind of person you are, what you value in life, the traits you like in others and yourself, along with the traits you don't. Now, quite a few of the questionnaires I came across are pretty dull. Your favourite colour, what are you scared of, what do you need to let go, what matters most in your life. Even things like your star sign and the star signs of people who you value. I mean, who believes in that stuff, stars and moons and all that? I mean, I know they're real and exist, like. I've seen them with my own eyes and I'm sure you've seen them, too. For the record, as a diehard Capricorn, I love a crescent moon.

But I thought it was only right for our book to have a section of questions for you to unearth some things about yourself that you didn't know or didn't even think you knew. So here they are, and what I think they say about you...

WHAT IS YOUR FAVOURITE WORD?

A gentle half-volley, this one, to get you up and running. It might be a word you use every day or one that pops up now and again and brings a smile to your face.

Malheureusement. It means 'unfortunately' in French. I just think it rolls off the tongue beautifully and it sounds very different in my accent. I feel like I can be someone I'm not when I say it. French is that kind of language where everything sounds classy. I also like the word 'divn't', which means 'don't' in Ashingtonian. And 'canny' because it's canny (nice, good). 'Bonnie' is a nice word as well. It's like a non-intrusive way of saying 'pretty' – 'oh, she's bonnie'.

WHAT IS YOUR LEAST FAVOURITE WORD?

Now we're getting the juices flowing. On that, 'moist' comes up a lot as a word people hate. I don't much mind it. It's often something that triggers a bad response. Whenever I think of 'moist' I think of cake. Who doesn't like cake?

'Sleck', which means, like, muck or sludge. 'Look at all that sleck on your shoe.' There's also 'needle', for obvious reasons, and 'mayonnaise' since it's the taste of the devil. That, olives and gorgonzola. Oh, and blue cheese. It's just mould, right? I know people think I've got the palate of a child, but you can't be eating mould. That's hardly controversial, is it?

WHAT TURNS YOU ON?

Not like that. This isn't that kind of book. Intellectually, I mean, rather than aseptically.

Music. I love singing or listening to music before I play, or dancing in the kitchen with Harry, or singing as if I'm on stage. This is an odd one, but I love a stand-alone tree in a field. It makes me think it's special. It makes me imagine an army coming across a field and having that tree as a focal point. That fresh smell of home. Not grass and stuff because I've got hay fever. But that familiar scent of air.

WHAT TURNS YOU OFF?

I'll accept mullets for this.

Selfishness, arrogance, alcohol, spice, funky menus or taster menus – they're just pointless. The ones that use ingredients that are over the top. Just keep it simple. For example, once, at Durham, we had pork tikka masala. Why? Just have pork and chicken tikka. It's just getting funky for no reason. Taster menus though, awful. Overpriced, they don't fill you up and they have stupid stuff like mushroom tartar. Crap.

WHAT SOUND DO YOU LOVE?

Think of a noise that lifts you. Like if you were a dog, I'd imagine it'd be the opening of the front door. They go mad for that.

The wood pigeons at home is a favourite as they'll always come out at the start of summer and that'll mean it's the cricket season. We had one that lived in the garden and it'd wake us up regularly during the season. The waves on the beach whenever we're in the Caribbean – that's incredibly relaxing. One noise that really gets me is the delayed cheer of a crowd. It's not the cheer itself but the split second of silence before they realize what's happened. I think what I love about it is that in that moment, only you know what's happened: whether it's when you see you're about to bowl someone, they've nicked it and it's going towards someone in the slip cordon or you've just sweetly connected with the bat and know it's a boundary. I've probably heard more of that last one when I've been bowling, to be honest. Never mind. I like Sam Billings' posh laugh ('UH-HUH UH-HUH UH-HUH'). Also, *The Last of the Mohicans* theme tune is a belter.

WHAT SOUND OR NOISE DO YOU HATE?

Something that makes you wince. Maybe it's someone's voice or the way they talk. Accents are usually a pet peeve for some people. Not mine, of course.

Boy racers, specifically the sound of their overly souped-up engines. Pointless. The feedback of a guitar and the worst, by a country mile, polystyrene when you're unwrapping stuff. The noise and the feel… honestly, I hate that more than anything. It sends shivers through me body. Horrible stuff, squeaky, dry. Bleugh. It's annoying because you get sent so much kit as a cricketer and a lot of it is packed with polystyrene.

WHO WOULD PLAY YOU IN A FILM?

Perfect for gauging how high you think of yourself. Like, if you're a bloke and picking Brad Pitt or Bradley Cooper – any Brad-type – you know you've got a big ego. The same for anyone really funny. And if you're picking more than one, well…

There's probably not one man who could do the job well enough, to be honest, so I've got four. Todd Armstrong who was Jason in *Jason and the Argonauts*. Just an absolutely belting film, so he's in. Sean Connery, because he's the best James Bond. He is better than Craig. If he had the modern films, he'd be undoubtedly the best. I've also got Hugh Jackman, because he likes cricket and when we were playing in Australia once, one fan went, 'Oi mate, are you Hugh Jackman's brother?' I'll take that. I didn't even think of it as a sledge. And lastly, Arnold Schwarzenegger, because he's got the best lines from the best films. There's that one from *Commando* where he's like, 'Matrix –

remember when I said I'd kill you last? I lied!' And then knocks him off the cliff. Imagine that before running in to bowl: 'Kohli – remember when I said I'd get you out last? I lied!' Then pin him back. I don't know how Arnie would get his arm over his shoulder with those deltoids. But I think all them four could fill the role of playing me nicely, for different reasons. We might need a big budget, mind, but I'm sure they'll happily split the fee four ways.

HOW DO YOU MEND A BROKEN HEART?

Technically a trick question as there are no wrong answers to this.

Ask Jimmy Ruffin, who recorded the classic song 'What Becomes of the Brokenhearted'.

IF YOUR CURRENT CAREER WAS NOT AN OPTION, WHAT WOULD YOU BE AND WHY?

A good one, I think, because it gets you thinking about how your skills apply to the real world. I think a lot of people, athletes included, think after a while they are so specialized in what they do that doing anything else seems quite daunting.

Well, I went to Newcastle College and got a foundation degree with a view to becoming a PE teacher. But that's still sport, isn't it? [*It is, yeah.*]. Well, I like history, so it'd have been cool to be part of a historical team, particularly around battles and warfare. Along the same lines, I always had an ambition of being a professional Viking. Just doing Viking things for people that needed them done. Like a contractor, but a Viking. I like Bamburgh Castle and the Vikings were involved in that, though I think they destroyed it, mind. I've also mastered the shield wall, as my batting shows. Then again, Vikings don't have the best reputation as being good blokes, so that's potentially a problem. Can you get a nice Viking?

WHAT PROFESSION OTHER THAN YOUR OWN WOULD YOU LIKE TO ATTEMPT?

Not related to your skills at all, but your interests. If you could build a new working life for yourself, how would it look? Perhaps a dream you always had but didn't go through with because you didn't think it was realistic or never had the opportunity to pursue. Or maybe something you'd want to experience.

If it's only for one day, I would like to be a miner. Just to go through what everyone like my grandad talks about all the time, and get first-hand experience of the hardship of my roots. I mean, I wouldn't enjoy it, but it would be nice to go through it and have that connection to it, just to get a better understanding of what it was actually like. On the other hand, I'd always dreamed about the football career I'd want to have. In fact, I've mapped it out completely. Strap yourselves in…

Obviously, I start at Ashington Football Club and I ply my trade as a centre midfielder, because that's my best position. Then I move to AFC Wimbledon in League Two, who have scouted us as a right-back. Why right-back, you ask? Because it's the only way I can get into the team. Bear in mind, I'm a young player, just getting into the rigours of league football. Can't do anything crazy like put myself in as a starter and with the captain's armband, can I? Even if this is all made up. And because I'm a good team player, I fill in there. The following season, Neal Ardley becomes manager and moves me to my correct position in centre midfield. Neal is one of my footballing heroes and he actually managed Wimbledon in the past, so he's come back. We hit it off straight away: I'm man of the match in a preseason friendly against Real Madrid and I never look back. In fact, I'm man of the match every game that season as Wimbledon get promoted to the Championship.

I'm given the captaincy the next season – it was coming, of course it was – and I attract a certain Glen Taylor from Spennymoor Town as centre forward. Glen scores 30 goals that campaign and I set up 29 of them. The only one I didn't get an assist for was for a penalty, which I actually won. We get up to the Premier League and by now I am in charge of transfer dealings because I have become that iconic with the club. Also, because I'm one of the most knowledgeable people when it comes to the best players on *Championship Manager 2000/01*. We go on to win the FA Cup against

Liverpool, like the 1988 FA Cup final. I, of course, score from a free kick. It's at that point that assistant manager Vinnie Jones asks us to go acting with him and, not going to lie, I'm tempted. Instead, I go on a big-money move to Inter Milan, because I've always liked them because they were blue and I always used to play as them on *Sensible Soccer*. I win the Scudetto in my first season. After various titles, including the Champions League, I move into the twilight years of my career at Rangers, following the footsteps of other great midfield players like Graeme Souness and Gazza.

WHAT PROFESSION WOULD YOU NOT LIKE TO DO?

What do you think is beyond your expertise or skills? Identify the environment you think you'd be less effective in. The kind of job that would have you pushing the alarm clock to the limit or even calling in sick. I've not done that much, but I have got a pretty good 'flu voice'.

I think I'd struggle to work by myself. I'd definitely need to work with people. I wouldn't like just being stuck in an office cubicle, I'd want to be able to converse with people and be a bit creative. I wouldn't like to be a lighthouse keeper. You'd drive yourself mad, wouldn't you? Also, have you seen the North Sea? You'd be on edge, wouldn't you, worried about all the ships coming to shore on your watch. I'd end up like Tom Hanks on *Castaway*, making friends with inanimate objects. Not good.

YOU'VE GOT A LAST-MINUTE TRIP TO THE AIRPORT AND YOU CAN'T DRIVE. WHICH OF YOUR COLLEAGUES IS MOST LIKELY TO GIVE YOU A LIFT?

Now, this one is tough because it's a real test of how well you think you get on with the people you work with. We all like to think we get on with our coworkers and vice versa, but this is a good way of seeing who you trust and who you might return the favour for.

Straight away, don't even need to think about it – Jonny Bairstow. He's dependable and goes the extra mile. For my wedding, he went to a wedding in Cardiff the night before, finished there at 1 a.m. and then got a car up to mine to be there. That was great dedication. He's got a heart of gold.

JONNY BAIRSTOW: *I was down in Chepstow in Wales, and his wedding was in Northumberland. I left this wedding at 1 a.m. and then arrived in Northumberland at 6.30 a.m. that morning. I had an hour's sleep, showered and changed for his wedding. Fresh suit, fresh shirt, fresh tie. Except he didn't tell me the heaters were on in the reception bit where they had the ceremony. So I was wearing a cardigan as well as the suit, so let's just say I was rather warm. We were cutting a few shapes on the dance floor later that evening, don't you worry.*

Jonny's also in the north anyway, so it's not too far. And he's got good taste in music so I wouldn't mind him plugging in his own playlist. Unlike Stokesy.

In terms of distance, Stokesy is probably the closest teammate, but I learned he's not the best company on a drive when we car-shared in 2015. And it's largely down to his music choices. He always likes to play anything modern, but the kind that gives you a thumping headache. You know if you did some form of exercise and your heart rate was between 140 and 200 beats per minute? That's the kind of music he listens to. I don't know why he needs to bother drinking Red Bull when he's got that pumping through his ears. During my section to drive he was going to sleep (somehow), so I figured if he's going to doze off, the proper etiquette is for me to choose what music I was listening to. 'Can I listen to my music?' I asked politely, when I shouldn't need to. 'No no no,' he protested, like one of his kids, I want to listen to this, this helps me go to sleep!' You must be a raging nutcase to try and fall asleep to this! I imagine if you were absolutely palatic in a nightclub, this would be the kind of music you'd like. He started to drift off and I managed to nick the cable. As I start to put it in my music, he woke up in a flash and started shouting, 'What the hell are you doing?!' I said he was being selfish. We ended up not speaking for the rest of the drive up. I think that's the only time I've fallen out with him.

BEN STOKES: *Woody, you're basically just deflecting here, because you're banned from being DJ in my car.*

MARK WOOD: *No, you're always falling asleep in situations like that. Do you remember that time you invited me around for a film in your room on tour? I thought, ah, this'll be nice, having some food and a bit of a chat while watching a movie. Within half an hour you were zonked. I drew the curtains, tucked you in and left the room.*

STOKES: *Yeah, OK fine. That was nice of you.*

WOOD: *Jonny it is.*

MARK WOOD, A SECOND OPINION

(by Miles Jupp)

was doing a show in Stockton-on-Tees and he came with his dad, his best mate and his best mate's dad. I remember being struck by that. 'You have probably all gone out together for the last twenty years,' I thought to myself. Of course, this night was no different in part because the man at the centre of it all – Mark Wood, World Cup winner, beloved international cricketer – is no different.

It might seem an unlikely person to compare him to, but he reminded me of Olivia Colman. I used to work with Olivia when she was already famous but much less famous than she is now. She hasn't changed at all in that time. You get that sense with Woody. Obviously, I didn't know him before he was 'Mark Wood – World Cup winner, beloved international cricketer'. But to see him at the theatre with his best mate and their dads, I thought, 'Oh yeah, you've not changed at all from doing this.' But that's who Woody reminds me of – Olivia Colman. Unchanged by success. And luckily, the thing he has not changed from is a really nice person.

For those who don't know, Mark and I have a podcast, *Middle Please, Umpire*. I went to the World Cup final and in one of the pictures of them on the stage you can see me in a blue shirt and a hat celebrating, holding the trophy up. That was previously the closest I'd been to him. Bizarrely, a few months later, I'm in a restaurant with him in King's Cross, just before recording our first episode with David Gower. Mark went up to settle the bill, came back and: 'Oh, and I've got everyone a pudding.'

Our producer Nathan Kosky had the idea during the first lockdown. My manager asked me, 'Do you want to make a podcast?' I said, no, not really. 'Well, it's about cricket.' Well, maybe. Then she revealed it would be me and Mark Wood and I thought, 'God, that will be amazing.' From my point of view, as someone in the stands, all these people are amazing. But he seems not quite like the others. I was sure it would be fun, and it was. We're very different but there was some kind of wavelength connection. I know loads of people like me. I love meeting people not like me.

There is no front to him. When you watch him on TV, he's got this game face. He is really just focused on what he has to do, but it is actually a slightly worried face. Of course it is – it is inconceivable somebody bowling that fast, especially as it is pretty much all through effort.

From a professional point of view, working with someone who is prepared to leap into silly stuff is a godsend. There was an episode of the podcast where he whistled the entirety of the *Antiques Roadshow* theme. The reason he did that was because he was trying to work out if he preferred that to the *University Challenge* theme tune, which he had whistled in its entirety moments before. He is open to that sort of thing and quite gloriously unpredictable.

The thing about someone who jokes and messes around a lot is it's rarely the only thing they're about. But it can be a thing on which people are judged very negatively. People associate people who make jokes with being troublemakers. Joke-making often is a coping mechanism, a way of putting a gloss on things. There is a protective element to it.

I think with someone like Woody, the injuries he has had, the injuries he has come back from – part of me thinks, would he be able to do that without very deliberately focusing on the lighter side of life? He's a man who has made so many sacrifices. Like a lot of them, his life is built around being able to do what he does at the highest possible level. To do that, to have the injuries, to have the rehab, to have done them before, know what it's like and keep going to the well, I think his capacity to be a bit wacky and silly must have made it so much easier to come back, compared to others who are injury-plagued. The work that goes into achieving what he has achieved is astonishing, it really is.

He is very self-critical. I remember talking to him after the bumper barrage against India at Lord's in the 2021 summer. England lost the Test and he was like, 'That's on me – I should have bowled them out. *I* am the person who should have bowled them out.' With some people, there is a lot of narcissism when it comes to self-criticism. But with him it comes from a constructive place because there is no entitlement to him. He seems very much of the mind that you have got to earn any success you have.

He is from an environment where if you want to do things then you have to work hard and hopefully you can do them. He's not someone who has any sense of divine right about it, and I think that's a strength of his. The way cricket is in this country, England lose and the reaction is: 'Well, I don't think they said we'd lose when we were at school. What's going on? I thought this was one of those things: we could be prime minister, we could win the Ashes. I don't understand how I'm sitting here in my socks having achieved neither. What were the fees for?' You get none of that with him.

This vulnerability of his is interesting because even that comes from a selfless place. My phone rang at 9.30 p.m. one night. I asked if he was all right. He had just parked up somewhere on the way back from Durham and was going, 'I just didn't bowl very well today. I'm embarrassed by it. If you're the international player and you don't turn up and bowl well, it's just embarrassing.' He then asked if I have ever played a local comedy club and it had not gone well. He imagined that's what it would feel like.

To me, it was very flattering for someone to be that open with you. You feel privileged, really, to have something like that shared with you, or that you might be the person he turns to because he wanted to find some sort of equivalence. I also thought it was fascinating that he clearly wanted to have this conversation before he got home. He wanted that to be dealt with, he didn't want to bring any of it into the house. He just wants to leave work at work. I thought it was very selfless of him because he could have gone home and moped.

I was quite struck by that conversation. Of course, these sports stars have feet of clay, but you don't usually see any of that. You know if you're doing a speech and say, 'God, I was nervous,' and someone says, 'Oh, you didn't look it.' That's half the battle, isn't it? Looking like you're meant to be there. Making a speech is terrifying but people book you to do one because they think it's a thing you can do without effort. And, as absurd as it is, I'm sure people look at Mark bowling close to 100 mph and think the same.

I have only known him for two or three years, but in that time I have had so many conversations with him. Just chats about, well, stuff, and I love his attitude. I guess it is the normalness and sincerity of the man. I feel that anyone Woody trusts or says is a good guy, I would be happy to take him on that word. I wouldn't need a secondary source to back that up. We all get on with some people that everyone else thinks are absolute maniacs, but I find

I implicitly trust him when it comes to people. Other than when he talks down about himself, I guess.

He's got a world around him – a real family and community – that holds him in good stead for being in a world that is very up and down, unpredictable, high pressure and all of those things. The other parts of his life are very solid and he is very rooted in where he is from. I can't ever imagine a headline saying 'MARK WOOD SIGNS FOR NOTTS!'

It's quite enviable, to have such a strong sense of identity. I'm envious of that. I'm a boarding-school person so you end up not knowing exactly where you're from. If someone asks you 'What's your home town?' it takes you ninety seconds to answer. My brother lives in Scotland, my parents live in the East Midlands and I live in Wales. I can't imagine Woody would ever be in that situation. He is exactly who he is and exactly from where he is, and those things are completely intertwined. He is genuinely grounded, genuinely earthed. Maybe in this self-help book, he should write: 'Don't move anywhere' – and certainly don't change who you are fundamentally. Both have worked pretty well for him.